P9-DWH-113

Why Do You Need This New Edition?

If you're wondering why you should buy this new edition of *Style: The Basics,* here are four good reasons:

1. A new chapter on global coherence replaces one on correctness, reflecting a greater focus throughout on creating a coherent and persuasive argument rather than on correcting individual errors.

2. A new discussion of critical reading, and an expanded emphasis on reading throughout, provide guidance for readers in understanding difficult texts—the first step in helping you become a better writer.

3. A revised Lesson 2 focuses more strongly on helping you make good decisions about questions of usage in your own writing.

4. Revised Lessons 5 and 6 emphasize the need to begin sentences with clear, straightforward language and to push grammatical complexity to the ends of sentences—a strategy that will help you reach your own readers more effectively.

PEARSON

STYLE

The Basics of Clarity and Grace

FOURTH EDITION

Joseph M. Williams (Late)
The University of Chicago

Revised by

Gregory G. Colomb
The University of Virginia

Longman

Boston   Columbus   Indianapolis   New York   San Francisco   Upper Saddle River
Amsterdam   Cape Town   Dubai   London   Madrid   Milan   Munich   Paris   Montreal   Toronto
Delhi   Mexico City   São Paulo   Sydney   Hong Kong   Seoul   Singapore   Taipei   Tokyo

Senior Sponsoring Editor: Virginia L. Blanford
Senior Marketing Manager: Sandra McGuire
Production Manager: Renata Butera
Project Coordination, Text Design,
    and Electronic Page Makeup: Chitra Ganesan, PreMediaGlobal
Creative Director: Jayne Conte
Cover Designer: Bruce Kenselaar
Cover: фон абстрактный © petrovod
Printer and Binder: Edwards Brothers
Cover Printer: Lehigh-Phoenix Color

Library of Congress Cataloging-in-Publication Data

Williams, Joseph M.
    Style : the basics of clarity and grace / Joseph M. Williams; revised by
    Gregory G. Colomb. — 4th ed.
        p. cm.
    Includes bibliographical references and index.
    ISBN-13: 978-0-205-83076-3 (alk. paper)
    ISBN-10: 0-205-83076-5 (alk. paper)
        1. English language—Rhetoric.   2. English language—Technical
English.   3. English language—Business English.   4. English
language–Style.   5. Technical writing.   6. Business writing.   I. Colomb,
Gregory G.   II. Title.
    PE1421.W5455 2010
    808'.042—dc22

                                                                    2010032819

Copyright © 2012, 2009, 2006 by Pearson Education, Inc.

All rights reserved. No part of this publication may be reproduced, stored
in a retrieval system, or transmitted, in any form or by any means, elec-
tronic, mechanical, photocopying, recording, or otherwise, without the
prior written permission of the publisher. Printed in the United States.

Longman
is an imprint of

PEARSON

2 3 4 5 6 7 8 9 10—EB—13 12 11

ISBN 13: 978-0-205-83076-3
ISBN 10:   0-205-83076-5

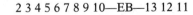

www.pearsonhighered.com

To my mother and father

. . . English style, familiar but not coarse,
elegant, but not ostentatious . . .
—SAMUEL JOHNSON

CONTENTS

PREFACE

Most people won't realize that writing is a craft.
You have to take your apprenticeship in it like anything else.
—KATHERINE ANNE PORTER

On February 22, 2008 the world lost a great scholar and teacher and I lost my dear friend Joe Williams. Though it should be Joe writing these words, I am honored to do it in his place. For this fourth edition of *Style: The Basics*, I have made only minor changes to most of the chapters, chiefly line editing. In a few places, I have indicated how students can use the advice about writing to help them read difficult prose. But I have also made one major change: I have replaced the chapter on correctness with a chapter on global coherence, which many teachers have said would be more useful.

Overall, this fourth edition aims at answering the same questions Joe asked in the first three, with one addition:

- What is it in a sentence that makes readers judge it as they do?
- How can we diagnose our own prose to anticipate their judgments?
- How can we revise a sentence so that readers will think better of it?
- How can we prepare readers so that they are better able to integrate all of our sentences into a coherent whole?

The standard advice about writing ignores those questions. It is mostly truisms like "Make a plan" and "Think of your audience"—advice that most of us ignore as we wrestle ideas onto the page. When we first draft a paragraph, we mostly struggle to get our own ideas straight. It is when we revise that we can think about our readers and discover what will serve them best. Some of us also know that as we revise, there are principles we can rely on to better anticipate how our readers will react. This book explains them.

PRINCIPLES, NOT PRESCRIPTIONS

These principles may seem prescriptive, but that's not how we intend them. We offer them as ways to help you predict how readers will judge your prose and then help you decide whether and how to revise it. As you learn these principles, you may find that you write more slowly. That's inevitable. Whenever we reflect on what we do as we do it, we become self-conscious, sometimes to the point of paralysis. It passes. You can avoid some of that paralysis if you remember that these principles have little to do with how you draft, much to do with how you revise. If there is a first principle of drafting, it's to forget all advice about how to do it.

To learn how to revise efficiently, though, you have to know a few things:

- You should know a few grammatical terms: subject, verb, noun, active, passive, clause, preposition, and coordination.
- You will have to learn new meanings for three familiar words: topic, stress, and theme.
- You will need five terms that you probably don't know. Two are important: nominalization and metadiscourse; three are useful: resumptive modifier, summative modifier, and free modifier.

Finally, if you are reading this book on your own, go slowly. It is not an amiable essay to read in a sitting or two. Take the lessons a few pages at a time. Practice by editing someone else's writing, then some of your old writing, then something you've written that day.

If you find these principles useful and would like a text that offers a fuller discussion of style as well as revision exercises, a longer version is available: *Style: Lessons in Clarity and Grace*, Tenth Edition. Order by using ISBN 0205747469.

ACKNOWLEDGMENTS

So many have offered support, suggestions, and criticisms over the last twenty-five years, that I cannot thank you all. Joe and I learned from thousands of undergraduate, graduate, and professional students, and post-docs who have gone through the Little Red Schoolhouse writing program (a.k.a. Advanced Academic and Professional Writing) at the University of Chicago, the University of Illinois, and the University of Virginia. We have been especially thankful to those graduate instructors who offered important criticisms and suggestions.

For several years, Joe and I had the good fortune to work closely with Don Freeman. Don's careful readings have saved this book from more than a few howlers.

Finally, a word about Joe's family. I saw almost daily how much they contributed to his life and sustained him in his work. Oliver, Michele, and Eleanor; Chris; Dave, Patty, Matilde, and Owen; Megan, Phil, Lily, and Calvin; Joe, Christine, Katherine, and Nicholas; and his beloved Joan. He loved you all more than he could say but not, I think, more than you knew.

My own family shared the blessings of knowing Joe but also suffered all those hours I spent working with him rather than being with them. For their patience and for giving meaning to that work, I thank Robin and Kiki, Karen, and Lauren. And Sandra remains the heart of it all, my love and companion for forty years.

G.G.C.
Charlottesville, Virginia

Understanding Style

Have something to say, and say it as clearly as you can.
That is the only secret of style.
—MATTHEW ARNOLD

CLARITY AND UNDERSTANDING

This book rests on two beliefs: it is good to write clearly, and anyone can do it. The first is self-evident, especially to those who read
a lot of writing like this:

> An understanding of the causal factors involved in excessive drinking
> by students could lead to their more effective treatment.

But that second belief may seem optimistic to those who want to
write clearly, but can't get close to this:

> We could more effectively treat students who drink too much if we
> understood why they do so.

It is a problem that has afflicted generations of writers who
have hidden their ideas not only from their readers but even from
themselves. When we read that kind of writing in government

regulations, we call it *bureaucratese;* in legal documents, *legalese;* in academic writing that inflates small ideas into gassy abstractions, *academese.* Written deliberately or carelessly, it is a language of exclusion that a democracy cannot tolerate.

THE IRRESISTIBLE LURE OF OBSCURITY

In the best-known essay on English style, "Politics and the English Language," George Orwell anatomized the turgid language of politicians, academics, and others:

> The keynote [of a pretentious style] is the elimination of simple verbs. Instead of being a single word, such as *break, stop, spoil, mend, kill,* a verb becomes a phrase, made up of a noun or adjective tacked on to some general-purposes verb such as *prove, serve, form, play, render.* In addition, the passive voice is wherever possible used in preference to the active, and noun constructions are used instead of gerunds (*by examination* of instead of *by examining*).

But in abusing that style Orwell adopted it. He could have written more concisely:

> Pretentious writers avoid simple verbs. Instead of using one word, such as *break, stop, kill,* they turn the verb into a noun or adjective, then tack onto it a general-purpose verb such as *prove, serve, form, play, render.* Whenever possible, they use the passive voice instead of the active, and noun constructions instead of gerunds (*by examination* instead of *by examining*).

If the best-known critic of a turgid style could not resist it, we shouldn't be surprised that politicians and academics embrace it. On the language of the social sciences:

> A turgid and polysyllabic prose does seem to prevail in the social sciences. . . . Such a lack of ready intelligibility, I believe, usually has little or nothing to do with the complexity of thought. It has to do almost entirely with certain confusions of the academic writer about his own status.

> —C. Wright Mills, *The Sociological Imagination*

On the language of medicine:

> It now appears that obligatory obfuscation is a firm tradition within the medical profession. . . . [Medical writing] is a highly skilled, calculated attempt to confuse the reader. . . . A doctor feels he might get passed over for an assistant professorship because he wrote his papers too clearly—because he made his ideas seem too simple.
>
> —Michael Crichton, *New England Journal of Medicine*

On the language of law:

> In law journals, in speeches, in classrooms and in courtrooms, lawyers and judges are beginning to worry about how often they have been misunderstood, and they are discovering that sometimes they can't even understand each other.
>
> —Tom Goldstein, *New York Times*

On the language of science:

> There are times when the more the authors explain [about ape communication], the less we understand. Apes certainly seem capable of using language to communicate. Whether scientists are remains doubtful.
>
> —Douglas Chadwick, *New York Times*

Most of us first confront that kind of writing in textbook sentences like this one:

> Recognition of the fact that systems [of grammar] differ from one language to another can serve as the basis for serious consideration of the problems confronting translators of the great works of world literature originally written in a language other than English.

In about half as many words, that means,

> When we recognize that languages have different grammars, we can consider the problems of those who translate great works of literature into English.

Generations of students have struggled with dense writing, many thinking they weren't smart enough to grasp a writer's deep ideas. Some have been right about that, but more could have blamed the writer's inability (or refusal) to write clearly. Many students, sad to say, give up; sadder still, others learn not only to read that style but write it, inflicting it in turn on their readers, thereby sustaining a 450-year-old tradition of unreadable writing.

SOME PRIVATE CAUSES OF UNCLEAR WRITING

Unclear writing is a social problem, but it often has private causes. Michael Crichton mentioned one: some writers plump up their prose, hoping that complicated sentences indicate deep thought. And when we want to hide the fact that we don't know what we're talking about, we typically throw up a tangle of abstract words in long, complex sentences.

Others write graceless prose not deliberately but because they are seized by the idea that good writing must be free of the kind of errors that only a grammarian can explain. They approach a blank page not as a space to explore ideas, but as a minefield of potential errors. They creep from word to word, concerned less with their readers' understanding than with their own survival.

Others write unclearly because they freeze up, especially when they are learning to think and write in a new academic or professional setting. As we struggle to master new ideas, most of us write worse than we do when we write about things that we understand. If that sounds like you, take heart: you will write more clearly when you more clearly understand what you are writing about.

But the biggest reason most of us write unclearly is that we don't know when readers will think we are unclear, much less why. Our own writing always seems clearer to us than to our readers, because we read into it what we want them to get out of it. And so instead of revising our writing to meet our readers' needs, we send it off the moment it meets ours.

In all of this, of course, is a great irony: we are likely to confuse others when we write about a subject that confuses us. But when we become confused by a complex style, we too easily

~~assume that its complexity signals deep thought, and so we try to~~
~~imitate it, compounding our already-confused writing.~~

●N WRITING AN● REA●ING

This is a book about writing based on our ways of reading. Once you understand why you judge one sentence to be dense and abstract and another clear and direct, you will know how to recognize not only when others' writing is more complex than deep and but when yours may be as well. The problem is, none of us can judge our own writing as others will because we respond less to the words on the page than to the thoughts in our minds. You can avoid that trap once you learn how the words you have put *on the page* make *your readers* feel as they do.

You can also do something for yourself: The principles here also serve you as you read. When you encounter difficult prose, you will know what to look for on the page to determine whether your difficulty comes from the necessary complexity of the material or the gratuitous complexity of the writing. If the latter, use these principles to help you mentally revise the abstract and indirect writing of others into something you can better understand (while giving yourself the silent satisfaction of knowing that you could have written it more clearly).

ON WRITING AND REWRITING

A warning: If you think about these principles *as you draft*, you may never finish drafting. Most experienced writers get something down as fast as they can. Then as they rewrite that first draft into something clearer, they understand their ideas better. And when they understand their ideas better, they express them more clearly, and the more clearly they express them, the better they understand them . . . and so it goes, until they run out of energy, interest, or time.

For a fortunate few, that ending comes weeks, months, even years after they begin. For most of us, though, our deadline is closer to tomorrow morning. And so we have to settle for prose that is less than perfect, but as good as we can make it. (Perfection may be ideal, but it is the death of done.)

So use what you find here not as rules to impose on every sentence *as* you draft it, but as principles to help you identify sentences that might give your readers a problem, and then to revise them.

As important as clarity is, though, some occasions call for more:

> Now the trumpet summons us again—not as a call to bear arms, though arms we need; not as a call to battle, though embattled we are; but a call to bear the burden of a long twilight struggle, year in and year out, "rejoicing in hope, patient in tribulation," a struggle against the common enemies of man: tyranny, poverty, disease and war itself.
>
> —John F. Kennedy, Inaugural Address, January 20, 1961

Few of us are called upon to write a presidential address, but even on less lofty occasions, some of us take a private pleasure in writing a shapely sentence, even if no one will notice. If you enjoy not just writing a sentence but crafting it, you will find some ideas in Lesson 8. Writing is more than just adding one sentence after another, no matter how clear, so in Lesson 9 I suggest some ways to organize your sentence into a coherent whole. Writing is also a social act that might or might not serve the best interests of your readers, so in Lesson 10, I address some issues about the ethics of style.

Many years ago, H. L. Mencken wrote this:

> With precious few exceptions, all the books on style in English are by writers quite unable to write. . . . Their central aim, of course, is to reduce the whole thing to a series of simple rules—the overmastering passion of their melancholy order, at all times and everywhere.

Mencken was right: no one learns to write well by rule, especially those who cannot see or feel or think. But I know that many do see clearly, feel deeply, and think carefully but still cannot write sentences that make those thoughts, feelings, and visions clear to others. I also know that the more clearly we write, the more clearly we see and feel and think. Rules help no one do that, but some principles can. The first is to put your readers ahead of yourself:

> Essentially style resembles good manners. It comes of endeavouring to understand others, of thinking for them rather yourself—or thinking, that is, with the heart as well as the head.
>
> —Sir Arthur Quiller-Couch

Actions

Everything that can be thought at all can be thought clearly.
Everything that can be said can be said clearly.
—LUDWIG WITTGENSTEIN

UNDERSTANDING HOW WE MAKE JUDGMENTS

We have words enough to praise the writing we like: *clear, direct, concise,* and more than enough to abuse what we don't: *unclear, indirect, abstract, dense, complex.* We can use those words to distinguish these two sentences:

> 1a. The cause of our schools' failure at teaching basic skills is not understanding the influence of cultural background on learning.

> 1b. Our schools have failed to teach basic skills because they do not understand how cultural background influences the way a child learns.

Most of us would call (1a) dense and complex and (1b) clearer, more direct. But those words don't refer to anything *in* those sentences; they describe how those sentences make us *feel.* When we say that (1a) is *unclear,* we mean that *we* had a hard time understanding it; we say it's *dense* when *we* have to struggle through it.

The problem is to understand what is *in* those two sentences that makes readers feel as they do. Only then can you rise above your too-good understanding of your own writing to know when readers will think it needs revising. To do that, you have to know what counts as a well-told story.

TELLING STORIES ABOUT CHARACTERS AND THEIR ACTIONS

It is easy to state the most general principle for clear sentences: Make the main character in your sentence its subject and make its important actions verbs. This story doesn't do that:

> 2a. Once upon a time, as a walk through the woods was taking place on the part of Little Red Riding Hood, the Wolf's jump out from behind a tree occurred, causing her fright.

We prefer a sentence closer to this:

> ✓ 2b. Once upon a time, Little Red Riding Hood was walking through the woods, when the Wolf jumped out from behind a tree and frightened her.

Most readers think (2b) tells its story more clearly than (2a), because it follows two principles that (2a) ignores:

- Its main characters are subjects of verbs.
- Those verbs express specific actions.

Principle of Clarity 1: Make Main Characters Subjects

Look at the subjects in (2a). The simple subjects (boldfaced) are *not* the main characters (italicized):

> 2a. Once upon a time, as a **walk** through the woods was taking place on the part of *Little Red Riding Hood*, *the Wolf's* **jump** out from behind a tree occurred, causing *her* fright.

Those subjects do not name characters; they name actions expressed in abstract nouns, *walk* and *jump:*

SUBJECT	VERB
a **walk** through the woods	was taking place
the *Wolf's* **jump** out from behind a tree	occurred

The whole subject of *occurred* does have a character in it: *the* **Wolf's** *jump,* but *the Wolf* is not the simple subject. It is only attached to the simple subject *jump.*

Contrast those abstract subjects with these, where the characters (italicized) are also the simple subjects (boldfaced):

> ✓ 2b. Once upon a time, ***Little Red Riding Hood*** was walking through the woods, when ***the Wolf*** jumped out from behind a tree and frightened *her.*

Principle of Clarity 2: Make Important Actions Verbs

Now look at how the actions and verbs differ in (2a): its actions (boldfaced) are not in verbs (capitalized):

> 2a. Once upon a time, as a **walk** through the woods WAS TAKING place on the part of Little Red Riding Hood, the Wolf's **jump** out from behind a tree OCCURRED, causing **her fright.**

Note how vague those verbs are: *was taking, occurred.* In (2b), the clearer sentence, the verbs name specific actions:

> ✓ 2b. Once upon a time, Little Red Riding Hood WAS WALKING through the woods, when the Wolf JUMPED out from behind a tree and FRIGHTENED her.

Here's the point: In (2a) and (2b), the two main characters are Little Red Riding Hood and the Wolf. In the wordy and indirect sentence, (2a), they are *not* subjects, and their actions—*walk, jump,* and *fright*—are *not* verbs. In the more direct sentence, (2b), those characters are subjects and their actions are verbs. That's why we prefer (2b).

FAIRY TALES AND ACADEMIC WRITING

Fairy tales may seem distant from writing in college or on the job, but they're not, because most sentences are still about characters doing things. Compare these two:

> 3a. The Federalists' argument in regard to the destabilization of government by popular democracy was based on their belief in the tendency of factions to further their self-interest at the expense of the common good.

> ✓ 3b. The Federalists argued that popular democracy destabilized government, because they believed that factions tended to further their self-interest at the expense of the common good.

We can analyze those sentences as we did the ones about Little Red Riding Hood.

Sentence (3a) feels dense for two reasons. First, its characters are not subjects. The simple subject (underlined) is *argument,* but the characters (italicized) are *Federalists, popular democracy, government,* and *factions*:

> 3a. *The Federalists'* <u>argument</u> in regard to the destabilization of *government* by *popular democracy* was based on *their* belief in the tendency of *factions* to further *their* self-interest at the expense of the common good.

Second, most of the actions (boldfaced) are not verbs (capitalized), but abstract nouns. And neither verb is an action.

> 3a. The Federalists' **argument** in regard to the **destabilization** of government by popular democracy WAS BASED on their **belief** in the **tendency** of factions to FURTHER their self-interest at the expense of the common good.

Notice the long, complex subject of (3a) and how little meaning is expressed by its main verb *was based:*

WHOLE SUBJECT	VERB
The Federalists' argument in regard to the destabilization of government by popular democracy	was based

Readers think (3b) is clearer for two reasons: first, its characters (italicized) are subjects (underlined) and its actions (boldfaced) are verbs (capitalized).

> 3b. The *Federalists* ARGUED that *popular democracy* DESTABILIZED government, because *they* BELIEVED that *factions* TENDED TO FURTHER *their* self-interest at the expense of the common good.

Note as well that all those whole subjects are short, specific, and concrete:

WHOLE SUBJECT/CHARACTER	VERB/ACTION
the Federalists	argued
popular democracy	destabilized
they	believed
factions	tended to further

In the rest of this lesson, we look at actions and verbs; in the next, at characters and subjects.

VERBS AND ACTIONS

Our principle is this: *A sentence seems clear when its important actions are in verbs.* Look at how sentences (4a) and (4b) express their actions. In (4a), the actions (boldfaced) are not verbs (capitalized); they are nouns:

> 4a. Our **lack** of data PREVENTED **evaluation** of our **actions** in **targeting** funds to areas in **need** of **assistance**.

In (4b), on the other hand, the actions are almost all verbs:

> ✓ 4b. Because we LACKED data, we could not EVALUATE whether we HAD TARGETED funds to areas that NEEDED assistance.

Readers will think your writing is dense if you use lots of abstract nouns, especially those derived from verbs and adjectives, nouns ending in *-tion, -ment, -ence,* and so on, especially when you make those abstract nouns the subjects of verbs.

A noun derived from a verb or adjective has a technical name: *nominalization.* The word illustrates its meaning: when we nominalize the verb *nominalize,* we create the nominalization *nominalization.* A few examples:

VERB	→	NOMINALIZATION	ADJECTIVE	→	NOMINALIZATION
discover	→	discovery	careless	→	carelessness
resist	→	resistance	different	→	difference
react	→	reaction	proficient	→	proficiency

We can also nominalize a verb by adding *-ing* (making it a gerund):

She flies → her flying   We sang → our singing

Some nominalizations and verbs are identical:

hope → hope   result → result   repair → repair

We REQUEST that you REVIEW the data.

Our **request** is that you conduct a **review** of the data.

(Some actions also hide out in adjectives: *It is applicable → it applies.* Some others: *indicative, dubious, argumentative, deserving.*)

Here's the point: In grade school, we learned that subjects *are* characters (or "doers") and that verbs *are* actions. That's often true:

subject	verb	object
We	discussed	the problem.
doer	action	

But it is not true for this almost synonymous sentence:

subject	verb		
The problem	was	the topic	of our discussion.
		doer	action

We can move characters and actions around in a sentence, and subjects and verbs don't have to be any particular thing at all. But when in most of your sentences you put characters in subjects and actions in verbs, readers are likely to think your prose is clear, direct, and readable.

No element of style more characterizes turgid academic and professional writing, writing that feels abstract, indirect, and difficult than lots of nominalizations, *especially in the subjects of verbs.*

DIAGNOSIS AND REVISION: CHARACTERS AND ACTIONS

You can use the principles of verbs as actions and subjects as characters to explain why your readers judge your prose as they do. More important, you can also use them to identify and revise sentences that seem clear to you but will not to your readers. Revision is a three-step process: diagnose, analyze, and rewrite.

1. **Diagnose**
   a. Ignoring short (four- or five-word) introductory phrases, underline the first seven or eight words in each sentence.

      <u>The outsourcing of high-tech work to Asia</u> by corporations means the loss of jobs for many American workers.

   b. Then look for two results:
      - You underlined abstract nouns as simple subjects.

        The **<u>outsourcing</u>** <u>of high-tech work to Asia</u> by corporations means the loss of jobs for many American workers.

      - You underlined seven or eight words before getting to a verb.

        <u>The outsourcing of high-tech work to Asia</u> by corporations (10 words) MEANS the loss of jobs for many American workers.

2. **Analyze**
   a. Decide who your main characters are, particularly flesh-and-blood ones (more about this in the next lesson).

      The outsourcing of high-tech work to Asia by **corporations** means the loss of jobs for **many American workers.**

b. Then look for the actions that those characters perform, especially actions in those abstract nouns derived from verbs.

> The **outsourcing** of high-tech work to Asia by corporations means the **loss** of jobs for many American workers.

3. **Rewrite**
   a. If the actions are nominalizations, make them verbs.

   > outsourcing → outsource   loss → lose

   b. Make the characters the subjects of those verbs.

   > corporations outsource   American workers lose

   c. Rewrite the sentence with subordinating conjunctions such as *because, if, when, although, why, how, whether,* or *that.*

   > Many middle-class American workers are losing their jobs, **because** corporations are outsourcing their high-tech work to Asia.

Some Common Patterns

You can quickly spot and revise five common patterns of nominalizations.

1. **The nominalization is the subject of an empty verb such as *be, seems, has,* etc.:**

   > The **consideration** of the issue by the committee OCCURRED last week.

   a. Change the nominalization to a verb:

   > consideration → consider

   b. Find a character that would be the subject of that verb:

   > The **consideration** of the issue by *the committee* OCCURRED last week.

   c. Make that character the subject of the verb:

   > *The committee* CONSIDERED the issue last week.

2. **The nominalization follows an empty verb:**

   ✓ The *agency* CONDUCTED an **investigation** into the matter.

   a. Change the nominalization to a verb:

      investigation → investigate

   b. Replace the empty verb with the new verb:

      conducted → investigated

   The *agency* **INVESTIGATED** the matter.

3. **One nominalization is a subject of an empty verb and a second nominalization follows it:**

   <u>Our **loss** in sales</u> WAS a result of their **expansion** of outlets.

   a. Revise the nominalizations into verbs:

      loss → lose   expansion → expand

   b. Identify the characters that would be the subjects of those verbs:

      Our **loss** in sales WAS a result of *their* **expansion** of outlets.

   c. Make those characters subjects of those verbs:

      we lose   they expand

   d. Link the new clauses with a logical connection:
      • To express simple cause: *because, since, when*
      • To express conditional cause: *if, provided that, so long as*
      • To contradict expected causes: *though, although, unless*

      We **LOST** sales because *they* **EXPANDED** *their* outlets.

4. **A nominalization follows *there is* or *there are:***

   There IS no **need** for *our* further **study** of this problem.

   a. Change the nominalization to a verb:

      need → need   study → study

b. Identify the character that should be the subject of the verb:

> There IS no **need** for *our* further **study** of this problem.

c. Make that character the subject of the verb:

> no need → we need not   our study → we study

> *We* NEED not STUDY this problem further.

5. **Two or three nominalizations in a row are joined by prepositions:**

> We did a **review** of the **evolution** of the brain.

a. Turn the first nominalization into a verb:

> review → review

b. Either leave the second nominalization as it is, or turn it into a verb in a clause beginning with *how* or *why:*

> evolution of the brain → how the brain evolved

> First, *we* REVIEWED the **evolution** of the *brain.*

> ✓ First, *we* REVIEWED how *the brain* EVOLVED.

SOME HAPPY CONSEQUENCES

When you consistently rely on verbs to express key actions, your readers benefit in many ways:

1. Your sentences are more concrete. Compare:

> There WAS an affirmative **decision** for **expansion.**

> ✓ *The director* DECIDED to EXPAND the program.

2. Your sentences are more concise. When you use nominalizations, you have to add articles like *a* and *the* and prepositions such as *of, by,* and *in.*

> A **revision** *of* the program WILL RESULT *in* **increases** *in* our **efficiency** *in the* **servicing** *of* clients.

✓ If we **REVISE** the program, we **CAN SERVE** clients more **EFFICIENTLY**.

3. The logic of your sentences is clearer. When you nominalize verbs, you have to link actions with fuzzy prepositions and phrases such as *of, by,* and *on the part of.* But when you use verbs, you link clauses with subordinating conjunctions that spell out your logic, such as *because, although,* and *if:*

> Our more effective presentation of our study resulted in our success, despite an earlier start by others.
>
> ✓ **Although** others started earlier, we succeeded **because** we presented our study more effectively.

4. Your sentence tells a more coherent story. Nominalizations let you distort the sequence of actions. (The numbers refer to the real sequence of events.)

> Decisions[4] in regard to administration[5] of medication despite inability[2] of an irrational patient appearing[1] in a Trauma Center to provide legal consent[3] rest with the attending physician alone.

When you revise those actions into verbs and reorder them, you get a more coherent narrative:

> ✓ When a patient appears[1] in a Trauma Center and behaves[2] so irrationally that he cannot legally consent[3] to treatment, only the attending physician can decide[4] whether to medicate[5] him.

A Qualification: Useful Nominalizations

I have so relentlessly urged you to turn nominalizations into verbs that you might think you should never use them. But in fact, you can't write well without them. The trick is to know which nominalizations to keep and which to revise. Keep these:

1. **A nominalization is a short subject that refers to a previous sentence:**

> ✓ **These arguments** all depend on a single unproven claim.
> ✓ **This decision** can lead to positive outcomes.

Those nominalizations link one sentence to another in a cohesive flow, an issue I'll discuss in detail in Lesson 4.

2. **A short nominalization replaces an awkward** *The fact that:*

> The fact that she ADMITTED her guilt impressed me.
>
> ✓ Her **acknowledgment** of her guilt impressed me.

But then, why not this:

> ✓ *She* IMPRESSED me when *she* ADMITTED her guilt.

3. **A nominalization names what would be the object of the verb:**

> I accepted *what she* REQUESTED [that is, *She requested* **something**].
>
> ✓ I accepted her **request.**

4. **A nominalization refers to a concept so familiar that readers think of it as a character (more on this in Lesson 2):**

> ✓ Few problems have so divided us as **abortion** on **demand.**
>
> ✓ The Equal Rights **Amendment** was an issue in past **elections.**
>
> ✓ **Taxation** without **representation** did not spark the American **Revolution.**

You must develop an eye for distinguishing nominalizations that express a familiar idea from those that you can revise into a verb:

> There is a **demand** for a **repeal** of the car tax.
>
> ✓ We DEMAND that the government REPEAL the car tax.

Shakespeare's Hamlet had acting style in mind when he told the actors in the play-within-the-play how they should act their parts, but his advice also applies to how we should write our sentences:

> Suit the action to the word, the word to the action.
>
> —*Hamlet*, 3.2

Lesson

3

Characters

When character is lost, all is lost.

—ANONYMOUS

UNDERSTANDING THE IMPORTANCE OF CHARACTERS

Readers think sentences are clear and direct when they see key actions in their verbs. Compare (1a) with (1b):

> 1a. The CIA feared the president would recommend to Congress that it reduce its budget.
>
> 1b. The CIA had fears that the president would send a recommendation to Congress that it make reductions in its budget.

Most readers think (1a) is clearer than (1b), but not much. Now compare (1b) and (1c):

> 1b. The CIA had fears that the president would send a recommendation to Congress that it make reductions in its budget.

20

1c. The fear of the CIA was that a recommendation from the president to Congress would be for reductions in its budget.

Every reader thinks that (1c) is much less clear than either (1a) or (1b).

The reason is this: in both (1a) and (1b), important characters (italicized) are short, specific subjects (underlined) of verbs (capitalized):

1a. *The CIA* FEARED *the president* WOULD RECOMMEND to *Congress* that *it* REDUCE *its* budget.

1b. *The CIA* HAD fears that *the president* WOULD SEND a recommendation to *Congress* that *it* MAKE a reduction in *its* budget.

But in (1c), the two simple subjects (underlined) are not concrete characters but abstractions (boldfaced).

1c. The **fear** of the *CIA* WAS that **a recommendation** from the *president* to *Congress* WOULD BE for **reductions** in its budget.

The different verbs in (1a) and (1b) make some difference, but the abstract subjects in (1c) make a bigger one.

Here's the point: Readers want actions in verbs, but even more they want characters as subjects. We give readers a problem when for no good reason we do not name characters in subjects, or worse, delete them entirely, like this:

There was fear that there would be a recommendation for a budget reduction.

Who fears? Who recommends? Who reduces? It is important to express actions in verbs, but the *first* principle of a clear style is this: Make the subjects of most of your verbs the main characters in your story.

DIAGNOSIS AND REVISION: CHARACTERS

Finding and Relocating Characters

To get characters into subjects, you have to know three things:

1. when your subjects are not characters
2. if they aren't, where you should look for characters
3. what you should do when you find them (or don't)

For example, this sentence feels indirect and impersonal:

> Governmental intervention in fast-changing technologies has led to the distortion of market evolution and interference in new product development.

We can diagnose that sentence:

1. **Underline the first seven or eight words:**

   > <u>Governmental intervention in fast-changing technologies has</u> led to the distortion of market evolution and interference in new product development.

   In those first words, readers want to see characters not just *in* the whole subjects of verbs, as *government* is implied in *governmental,* but as their simple subjects. In that example, however, they aren't.

2. **Find the main characters.** They may be possessive pronouns attached to nominalizations, objects of prepositions (particularly *by* and *of*), or only implied. In that sentence, one main character is in the adjective *governmental;* the other, *market,* is in the object of a preposition: *of market evolution.*

3. **Skim the passage for actions involving those characters, particularly actions buried in nominalizations.** Ask *Who is doing what?*

governmental **intervention**	→ ✓	*government* **intervenes**
distortion	→ ✓	*[government]* **distorts**
market **evolution**	→ ✓	*markets* **evolve**
interference	→ ✓	*[government]* **interferes**
development	→ ✓	*[market]* **develops**

To revise, reassemble those new subjects and verbs into a sentence, using conjunctions such as *if, although, because, when, how,* and *why:*

✓ When a *government* **INTERVENES** in fast-changing technologies, *it* **DISTORTS** how *markets* **EVOLVE** or **INTERFERES** with *their* ability to **DEVELOP** new products.

Be aware that just as actions can be in adjectives (*reliable → rely*), so can characters:

Medieval *theological* debates often addressed issues considered trivial by modern *philosophical* thought.

When you find a character implied in an adjective, revise in the same way:

✓ *Medieval theologians* often debated issues that *modern philosophers* consider trivial.

> ***Here's the point:***   The first step in diagnosing your style is to look at your subjects. If you do not see your main characters as simple subjects, you have to look for them. They can be in objects of prepositions, in possessive pronouns, or in adjectives. Once you find them, look for actions they are involved in. When you are revising, make those characters the subjects of verbs naming those actions. When you are reading, try to retell the story of the passage in terms of those characters and their actions.

RECONSTRUCTING ABSENT CHARACTERS

Readers have the biggest problem with sentences devoid of characters:

A decision was made in favor of doing a study of the disagreements.

That sentence could mean either of these, and more:

We decided that I should study why they disagreed.

I decided that you should study why he disagreed.

The writer may know who is doing what, but readers might not and so usually need help.

Sometimes we omit characters to make a general statement.

> Research strategies that look for more than one variable are of more use in understanding factors in psychiatric disorder than strategies based on the assumption that the presence of psychopathology is dependent on a single gene or on strategies in which only one biological variable is studied.

But when we try to revise that into something clearer, we have to invent characters, then decide what to call them. Do we use *one* or *we,* or name a generic "doer"?

> ✓ If *one/we/you/researchers* are to understand what causes psychiatric disorder, *one/we/you/they* should use research strategies that look for more than one variable rather than assume that a single gene is responsible for psychopathology or adopt a strategy in which *one/we/you/they* study only one biological variable.

To most of us, *one* feels stiff, but *we* may be ambiguous because it can refer just to the writer, to the writer and others but not the reader, to the reader and writer but not others, or to everyone. And if you are not directly naming your reader, *you* is usually inappropriate.

But if you avoid both nominalizations and vague pronouns, you can slide into passive verbs (I'll discuss them in a moment):

> To understand what makes patients vulnerable to psychiatric disorders, strategies that look for more than one variable SHOULD BE USED rather than strategies in which it IS ASSUMED that a gene causes psychopathology or only one biological variable IS STUDIED.

This is a matter where judgment is important, but in general, look for the most specific character you can find.

Abstractions as Characters

So far, I've discussed characters as if they had to be flesh-and-blood people. But you can tell stories whose main characters are abstractions, including nominalizations, so long as you make them the subjects of verbs that state specific actions involving them. We might have solved the problem of the previous example with a different kind of character, the abstraction *study:*

✓ To understand what causes psychiatric disorder, <u>*studies*</u> should look for more than one variable rather than adopt a strategy in which <u>*they*</u> test only one biological variable or assume that <u>a single gene</u> is responsible for a psychopathology.

The term *studies* names a virtual character because we are so familiar with it and because it is the subject of a series of actions: *understand, should look, adopt, test,* and *assume.*

But when you do use abstractions as characters, you can create a problem. A story about an abstraction as familiar as *studies* is clear enough, but if you surround an unfamiliar abstract character with a lot of other abstractions, readers may feel that your writing is dense and complex.

For example, few of us are familiar with *prospective* and *immediate intention,* so most of us are likely to struggle with a story about them, especially when those terms are surrounded by other abstractions (actions are boldfaced; human characters are italicized):

> The **argument** is this. The cognitive component of **intention** exhibits a high degree of **complexity. Intention** is temporally **divisible** into two: prospective **intention** and immediate **intention.** The cognitive function of prospective **intention** is the **representation** of a *subject's* similar past **actions,** *his* current situation, and *his* course of future **actions.** That is, the cognitive component of prospective **intention** is a **plan.** The cognitive function of immediate **intention** is the **monitoring** and **guidance** of ongoing bodily **movement.**
>
> —Myles Brand, *Intending and Acting*

We can make that passage clearer if we tell its story from the point of view of flesh-and-blood characters (italicized; actions are boldfaced; verbs are capitalized):

✓ *I* ARGUE this about **intention. It** HAS a complex cognitive component of two temporal kinds: prospective and immediate. *We* USE prospective **intention** to REPRESENT how *we* HAVE ACTED in our past and present and how *we* WILL ACT in the future. That is, *we* USE the cognitive component of prospective **intention** to HELP *us* PLAN. *We*

USE immediate **intention** to MONITOR and GUIDE *our* bodies as *we* MOVE them.

But have I made this passage say something that the writer didn't mean? Some argue that any change in form changes meaning. In this case, the writer might offer an opinion, but only his readers could decide whether the two passages have different meanings, because at the end of the day, a passage means only what careful and competent readers think it does.

Here's the point: Most readers want subjects to name the main characters in a story and those main characters to be flesh-and-blood. But often, you must write about abstractions. When you do, turn them into virtual characters by making them the subjects of verbs that tell a story. If readers are familiar with your abstractions, no problem. But when they are not, avoid using lots of other abstract nominalizations around them. If the hidden characters are "people in general," try *we* or a general term for whoever is doing the action, such as *researchers, social critics, one,* and so on. But unlike many other languages, English has no good way to name a generic "doer."

CHARACTERS AND PASSIVE VERBS

More than any other advice, you probably remember *Write in the active voice, not in the passive.* That's not bad advice, but it has exceptions.

When you write in the active voice, you typically put

- the agent or source of an action in the subject
- the goal or receiver of an action in a direct object:

	subject	verb	object
Active:	I	lost	the money.
	character/agent	action	goal

The passive differs in three ways:

1. The subject names the goal of the action.
2. A form of *be* precedes a verb in its past participle form.
3. The agent or source of the action is in a *by*-phrase or dropped entirely:

	subject	be + verb	prepositional phrase
Passive:	The money	was lost	[by me].
	goal	action	character/agent

The terms *active* and *passive,* however, are ambiguous, because they can refer not only to those two grammatical constructions but to how those sentences make you *feel.* We call a sentence *passive* if it feels flat, regardless of whether its verb is grammatically in the passive voice.

For example, compare these two sentences.

We can manage problems if we control costs.

Problem management requires cost control.

Grammatically, both sentences are in the active voice, but the second *feels* passive, for three reasons:

- Neither of its actions—*management* and *control*—are verbs; both are nominalizations.
- The subject is *problem management,* an abstraction.
- The sentence lacks flesh-and-blood characters.

To understand why we respond to those two sentences as we do, we have to distinguish the literal meanings of *active* and *passive* from their figurative, impressionistic meanings.

Choosing Between Active and Passive

Some critics of style tell us to avoid the passive everywhere because it adds words and often deletes the agent, the "doer" of the action. But the passive is often the better choice. To choose between active and passive, you have to answer three questions:

1. **Must your readers know who is responsible for the action?** Often, we don't say who does an action, because we don't know or readers won't care. For example, we naturally choose the passive in these sentences:

   ✓ The president **WAS RUMORED** to have considered resigning.

   ✓ Those who **ARE FOUND** guilty can **BE FINED.**

   ✓ Valuable records should always **BE KEPT** in a safe.

   If we do not know who spread rumors, we cannot say. If no one doubts who finds people guilty, fines them, or should keep records safe, we don't have to say. So those passives are the right choice.

   Sometimes, of course, writers use the passive when they don't want readers to know who is responsible for an action, especially when it's the writer. For example,

   Since the test was not completed, the flaw was uncorrected.

   I will discuss the ethics of intended impersonality in Lesson 10.

2. **Would the active or passive verb help your readers move more smoothly from one sentence to the next?** We depend on the beginning of a sentence to give us a context of what we know before we read what's new. A sentence confuses us when it opens with information that is unexpected. For example, in the following passage, the subject of the second sentence gives us new and complex information (boldfaced), before we read familiar information that we recall from the previous sentence (italicized):

   We must decide whether to improve education in the sciences alone or to raise the level of education across the whole curriculum. **The weight given to industrial competitiveness as opposed to the value we attach to the liberal arts**_{new information} will determine_{verb} *our decision*_{familiar information}.

   In the second sentence, the verb *determine* is in the active voice: *will determine our decision.* But we could read the sentence more easily if it were passive, because the passive would put the short, familiar information (*our decision*) first and the newer, more complex information last, the order we prefer:

✓ We must decide whether to improve education in the sciences alone or raise the level of education across the whole curriculum.*Our decision*_{familiar information} WILL BE DETERMINED_{passive verb} **by the weight we give to industrial competitiveness as opposed to the value we attach to the liberal arts**_{new information}.

(I discuss the issue of old and new more extensively in the next lesson.)

3. **Would the active or passive give readers a more consistent and appropriate point of view?** The writer of this next passage reports the end of World War II in Europe from the point of view of the Allies. To do so, she uses active verbs to make the Allies a consistent sequence of subjects:

✓ By early 1945, *the Allies* HAD essentially DEFEATED_{active} Germany; all that remained was a bloody climax. *American, French, British, and Russian forces* HAD BREACHED_{active} its borders and WERE BOMBING_{active} it around the clock. But *they* HAD not yet so DEVASTATED_{active} Germany as to destroy its ability to resist.

Had she wanted to explain history from the point of view of Germany, she would have used passive verbs to make Germany the subject/character:

✓ By early 1945, *Germany* HAD essentially BEEN DEFEATED; _{passive} all that remained was a bloody climax. *Its borders* HAD BEEN BREACHED, _{passive} and *it* WAS BEING BOMBED _{passive} around the clock. *It* HAD not BEEN SO DEVASTATED _{passive,} however, that *it* could not RESIST.

Some writers switch from one character to another for no apparent reason. Avoid this:

✓ By early 1945, *the Allies* had essentially defeated Germany. *Its borders* had been breached, and *they* were bombing it around the clock. *Germany* was not so devastated, however, that *the Allies* would meet with no resistance. Though ***Germany's population*** was demoralized, ***the Allies*** still attacked their cities from the air.

Pick a point of view and stick to it.

> ***Here's the point:***   Many writers use the passive verb too often, but it is useful in these contexts:
>
> * You don't know who did an action, readers don't care, or you don't want them to know.
> * You want to shift a long bundle of information to the end of a sentence, especially when you can also move to its beginning a shorter chunk of more familiar information.
> * You want your readers to focus on a particular character.

The "Objective" Passive vs. I/We

Some scholarly writers claim that they cannot use a first-person subject because they must create an objective point of view, something like this:

> Based on the writers' verbal intelligence, prior knowledge, and essay scores, their essays **were analyzed** for structure and evaluated for richness of concepts. The subjects **were** then **divided** into a high- or low-ability group. Half of each group **was** randomly **assigned** to a treatment group or to a placebo group.

Contrary to that claim, academic and scientific writers use the active voice and the first-person *I* and *we* regularly. These passages come from articles in respected journals:

> ✓ This paper is concerned with two problems. How can **we** best handle in a transformational grammar certain restrictions that . . ., To illustrate, **we** may cite . . ., **we** shall show . . .
>
> ✓ Since the pituitary-adrenal axis is activated during the acute phase response, **we** have investigated the potential role . . ., Specifically, **we** have studied the effects of interleukin-1 . . .

Here are the first few words from several consecutive sentences from *Science,* a journal of great prestige:

✓ **We** examine . . ., **We** compare . . . , **We** have used . . ., Each has been weighted . . ., **We** merely take . . ., They are subject . . . , **We** use . . . , Efron and Morris describe . . ., **We** observed . . ., **We** might find . . .

> —John P. Gilbert, Bucknam McPeek, and Frederick Mosteller,
> "Statistics and Ethics in Surgery and Anesthesia," *Science*

It is not true that academic writers always avoid the first-person *I* or *we.*

Passives, Characters, and Metadiscourse

When academic writers do use the first person, however, they use it in with a specific kind of verb:

- They do use the first person with verbs that refer to the writer's own writing and thinking: *cite, show, inquire.* These verbs are often active and so in the first person: *We will show* . . . They are examples of what is called *metadiscourse.*

Metadiscourse is language that refers not to the substance of your ideas, but to yourself, your reader, or your writing:

– your thinking and act of writing: *We will explain, show, argue, claim, deny, suggest, contrast, add, expand, summarize* . . .

– your readers' actions: *consider now, as you recall, look at the next example* . . .

– the logic and form of what you have written: *first, second; to begin; therefore; however; consequently* . . . .

Metadiscourse appears most often in introductions, where writers announce their intentions: *I claim that* . . . , *I will show* . . . , *We begin by* . . . , and again at the end, when they summarize: *I have argued* . . . , *I have shown.* What distinguishes those actions is that only the writer can lay claim to them.

- On the other hand, scholarly writers generally *do not* use the first person with verbs that refer to specific actions they performed as part of their research, actions that anyone can perform: *measure, record, examine, observe, use.* Those verbs are usually in the passive voice: *The subjects were observed* . . .

We rarely find passages like this:

> To determine if monokines elicited an adrenal steroidogenic response, **I** ADDED preparations of . . .

Most writers would use a passive verb, *were added,* to name an action that anyone can perform, not just the writer:

> To determine if monokines elicited a response, **preparations of** . . . WERE ADDED.

But a problem lurks in a passive sentence like that: its writer dangled a modifier. You dangle a modifier when an introductory phrase has an *implied* subject that differs from the *explicit* subject in the following clause. In that example, the implied subject of the infinitive verb *determine* is *I* or *we: I determine* or *we determine.*

> [So that **I** could] determine if monokines elicited a response, preparations WERE ADDED.

But that *implied* subject, *I,* differs from the *explicit* subject of the clause it introduces— ***preparations** were added.* When the implied and explicit subjects differ, the modifier dangles. Writers of scientific prose use this pattern so often, though, that it has become standard usage in their community.

I might note that this impersonal "scientific" style is a modern development. In his "New Theory of Light and Colors" (1672), Sir Isaac Newton wrote this charming first-person account of an experiment:

> I procured a triangular glass prism, to try therewith the celebrated phenomena of colors. And for that purpose, having darkened my laboratory, and made a small hole in my window shade, to let in a convenient quantity of the sun's light, I placed my prism at the entrance, that the light might be thereby refracted to the opposite wall. It was at first a very pleasing diversion to view the vivid and intense colors produced thereby.

Here's the point: Some writers and editors avoid the first person by using the passive everywhere, but deleting an *I* or *we* doesn't make a researcher's thinking more objective. We know that behind those impersonal sentences are flesh-and-blood people doing, thinking, and writing. In fact, the first-person *I* and *we* are common in scholarly prose when used with verbs that name actions unique to the writer.

Noun + Noun + Noun

One more stylistic choice does not directly involve characters and actions, but I discuss it here because it can distort the match that readers expect between the form of an idea and the grammar of its expression. It is the long compound noun phrase:

> Early *childhood thought disorder misdiagnosis* often results from un-familiarity with recent *research literature* describing such conditions. This paper reviews seven recent studies in which are findings of particular relevance to *pre-adolescent hyperactivity diagnosis* and to *treatment modalities* involving *medication maintenance level evaluation procedures.*

Some grammarians claim we should never modify one noun with another, but that would rule out common phrases such as *stone wall, student center, space shuttle,* and many other useful terms.

But strings of nouns feel lumpy, so avoid them, especially ones you invent. When you find a compound noun of your own invention, revise, especially when it includes nominalizations. Just reverse the order of words and find prepositions to connect them:

early	childhood	thought	disorder
misdiagnosis	misdiagnose	disordered	thought
in early	childhood		

Reassembled, it looks like this:

> Physicians misdiagnose[5] disordered[4] thought[3] in young[1] children[2] because they are unfamiliar with recent literature on the subject.

If, however, a long compound noun includes a technical term in your field, keep that part of the compound and unpack the rest:

> Physicians misdiagnose[5] thought disorders[3,4] in young[1] children[2] because they are unfamiliar with recent literature on the subject.

At this point, you may be feeling overwhelmed by all these principles, maybe even wondering whether learning them is worth the effort. Samuel Taylor Coleridge would have thought so, because for him, clarity was a moral issue:

> Whatever is translatable in other and simpler words of the same language, without loss of sense or dignity, is bad.

Cohesion and Coherence

If he would inform, he must advance regularly from Things known to things unknown, distinctly without Confusion, and the lower he begins the better. It is a common Fault in Writers, to allow their Readers too much knowledge: They begin with that which should be the Middle, and skipping backwards and forwards, 'tis impossible for any one but he who is perfect in the Subject before, to understand their Work, and such an one has no Occasion to read it.
—BENJAMIN FRANKLIN

UNDERSTANDING CONNECTIONS

So far, I've discussed clarity as if we could achieve it just by mapping characters and actions onto subjects and verbs. But readers need more than individually clear sentences before they think a passage seems to "hang together." These two passages, for example, say much the same thing but feel different:

> 1a. The basis of our American democracy—equal opportunity for all— is being threatened by college costs that have been rising fast for the last several years. Increases in family income have been significantly outpaced by increases in tuition at our colleges and universities during

that period. Only the children of the wealthiest families in our society will be able to afford a college education if this trend continues. Knowledge and intellectual skills, in addition to wealth, will divide us as a people, when that happens. Equal opportunity and the egalitarian basis of our democratic society could be eroded by such a divide.

✓ 1b. In the last several years, college costs have been rising so fast that they are now threatening the basis of our American democracy— equal opportunity for all. During that period, tuition has significantly outpaced increases in family income. If this trend continues, a college education will soon be affordable only by the children of the wealthiest families in our society. When that happens, we will be divided as a people not only by wealth, but by knowledge and intellectual skills. Such a divide will erode equal opportunity and the egalitarian basis of our democratic society.

The first seems choppy, even disorganized; the second seems to hang together better.

But like the word *clarity*, the words *choppy* and *disorganized* refer not to the words on the page but to how they make us *feel*. What is it about the *arrangement* of words in (1a) that makes us feel we are moving through it in fits and starts? Why does (1b) seem to flow more easily? We base those judgments on two kinds of connections that make passages hang together:

- We judge sequences of sentences to be *cohesive* depending on how each sentence ends and the next begins.

- We judge a whole passage to be *coherent* depending on how all the sentences in a passage cumulatively begin. (In Lesson 9, we discuss coherence in whole documents.)

COHESION

The Sense of Flow

In Lesson 3, we devoted a few pages to that familiar advice, *Avoid passives*. If we always did, we would choose the active verb in sentence (2a) below over the passive in (2b):

2a. The collapse of a dead star into a point perhaps no larger than a marble $CREATES_{active}$ a black hole.

2b. A black hole **IS CREATED**$_{\text{passive}}$ by the collapse of a dead star into a point perhaps no larger than a marble.

But we might choose otherwise if we put those sentences into this passage:

> [1]Some astonishing questions about the nature of the universe have been raised by scientists studying black holes in space. [2a/b] [————]. [3]So much matter compressed into so little volume changes the fabric of space around it in puzzling ways.

Here's the active sentence there:

> 1a. [1]Some astonishing questions about the nature of the universe have been raised by scientists studying black holes in space. [2a]The collapse of a dead star into a point perhaps no larger than a marble creates a black hole. [3]So much matter compressed into so little volume changes the fabric of space around it in puzzling ways.

And here's the passive:

> 1b. [1]Some astonishing questions about the nature of the universe have been raised by scientists studying black holes in space. [2b]A black hole is created by the collapse of a dead star into a point perhaps no larger than a marble. [3]So much matter compressed into so little volume changes the fabric of space around it in puzzling ways.

Our sense of "flow" calls not for (2a), the sentence with the active verb, but for (2b), the one with the passive.

The reason is clear: the last four words of the first sentence introduce an important character—*black holes in space*. If we follow it with sentence (2a), the first concepts we hit are collapsed stars and marbles, information that seems to fall from the sky:

> [1] . . . universe have been raised by scientists **studying black holes in space. [2a]The collapse of a dead star into a point perhaps no larger than a marble** creates . . . .

But if we follow sentence (1) with the sentence with the passive verb, (2b), we connect those sentences more smoothly, because now the first words in (2b) repeat what we just read at the end of (1):

> [1] . . . studying **black holes in space.** [2b]**A black hole** is created by the collapse of . . .

Note too that the passive lets us put at the *end* of sentence (2b) words that connect it to the *beginning* of sentence (3):

> [1] . . . black holes in space. [2b]A black hole is created by the collapse of a dead star into **a point perhaps no larger than a marble.** [3]**So much matter compressed into so little volume** changes the fabric of space around it in puzzling ways.

Here's the point: Sentences are cohesive when the information in one appears in the first few words of the next. That gives us our experience of flow. And in fact, that's the biggest reason the passive is in the language: it lets us arrange sentences so that they flow easily from one to the next. We can integrate that insight with our principles about subject and characters, and verbs and actions.

Diagnosis and Revision: Old Before New

That principle of reading leads us to two principles of revising. They are mirror images. The first is this:

1. **Begin sentences with information familiar to your readers.** Readers get that familiar information from two sources. First, they remember words from the sentences they just read. That's why the beginning of sentence (2b) about black holes connects to the end of (1) and why the beginning of (3) connects to the end of (2b):

> [1] . . . questions about the nature of the universe have been raised by scientists studying **[black holes in space.** [2b]**A black hole]** is created by the collapse of a dead star into **[a point perhaps no larger**

than a marble. So much matter compressed into so little volume] changes the fabric of space . . .

Second, readers bring to a sentence a general knowledge of its content. We would not be surprised, for example, if a sentence (4) in that paragraph about black holes had begun like this:

> . . . changes the fabric of space around it in puzzling ways. [4]**Astronomers have reported** that . . .

The word *astronomers* did not appear in the preceding sentence, but since we are reading about space, we wouldn't be surprised by a reference to them.

The second principle is the flip side of the first.

2. **End sentences with information readers cannot predict.** Readers always prefer to read what's new *after* they read what's familiar.

You can more easily see when others fail to observe those principles in their writing than when you do, because after you've worked on your own ideas for a while, they all seem familiar—to you. But hard as it is to distinguish old from new in your own writing, you have to try, because readers want to begin sentences with information that is familiar to *them*, and only then move on to information that is new.

Here's the point: In every *sequence* of sentences, you have to balance principles that make individual sentences clear and principles that make a passage cohesive. *But in that tradeoff, give priority to helping readers create a sense of cohesive flow.* That means starting sentences with familiar information. Fortunately, this principle about old before new cooperates with the principle of characters as subjects. Once you mention your main characters, they become familiar to readers. So when you start with characters, you also start with familiar information.

COHERENCE

The Sense of the Whole

When you create cohesive flow, you take the first step toward helping readers feel that your prose hangs together. But they will judge you to be a competent writer only when they feel that your writing is not just cohesive but *coherent,* a quality different from cohesion. It's easy to confuse the words *cohesion* and *coherence* because they sound alike.

- Think of *cohesion* as pairs of sentences fitting together the way individual pieces of a jigsaw puzzle do (recall the black hole sentences).

- Think of *coherence* as seeing what all the sentences in a piece of writing add up to, the way all the pieces in a puzzle add up to the picture on the box.

This next passage has good cohesive flow because we move from the end of each sentence to the next without a hitch:

Sayner, Wisconsin, is the snowmobile capital of the world. The buzzing of snowmobile engines fills the air, and their tanklike tracks crisscross the snow. The snow reminds me of Mom's mashed potatoes, covered with furrows I would draw with my fork. Her mashed potatoes usually make me sick—that's why I play with them. I like to make a hole in the middle of the potatoes and fill it with melted butter. This behavior has been the subject of long chats between me and my analyst.

Though its individual sentences are cohesive, that passage as a whole is incoherent. (It was created by six different writers, one of whom wrote the first sentence, with the other five sequentially adding one sentence, knowing only the immediately preceding one.) It is incoherent for three reasons:

1. The subjects of the sentences are entirely unrelated.
2. The sentences share no common "themes" or ideas.
3. The paragraph has no one sentence that states what the whole passage supports or explains.

Subjects, Topics, and Grammar

For five hundred years, English teachers have defined *subject* in two ways:

1. the "doer" of the action
2. what a sentence is "about," its main topic

In Lessons 2 and 3, we saw why that first definition doesn't work: the subjects of many sentences are actions: *The **explosion** was loud.*

But also flawed is that second definition: *A subject is what a sentence is about.* It is flawed because often, the subject of a sentence doesn't state its main topic, the idea that the rest of the sentence "comments" on. That "topicalizing" function can be performed by other parts of a sentence. For example, none of the main subjects in these sentences name their topics:

- The main subject of the next sentence (italicized) is *it*, but the topic of the sentence (boldfaced) is *your claim*, the object of the preposition *for*:

  It is impossible for **your claim** to be proved.

- The subject of this sentence is *I*, but its topic is *this question*, the object of *to*:

  In regard to **this question**, *I* believe more research is needed.

- The subject of this sentence is *it*, but its topic is *our proposal*, the subject of a verb in a subordinate clause:

  It is likely that **our proposal** will be accepted.

- The subject of this sentence is *no one*, but its topic is *such results*, a direct object shifted to the front for emphasis:

  Such results *no one* could have predicted.

Diagnosis and Revision: Topics

As with issues of clarity, you can't predict how readers will judge the flow of your writing just by reading it, because you know what it means too well. You must analyze it more objectively. This passage feels choppy, out of focus, even disorganized:

> Consistent ideas toward the beginnings of sentences help readers understand what a passage is generally about. A sense of coherence arises when a sequence of topics comprises a narrow set of related ideas. But the context of each sentence is lost by seemingly random shifts of topics. Unfocused paragraphs result when that happens.

Here's how to diagnose its problems and revise it. You can diagnose and revise your own writing in the same way.

1. **Diagnose**
   a. Underline the first five or six words of every sentence in a passage, stopping if you hit the main verb.
   b. If you can, underline the first five or six words of every clause in those sentences, both subordinate and main.

   > <u>Consistent ideas toward the beginnings of</u> sentences, especially in their subjects, help readers understand <u>what a passage</u> is generally about. A <u>sense of coherence</u> arises when <u>a sequence of topics</u> comprises a narrow set of related ideas. But <u>the context of each sentence</u> is lost by seemingly random shifts of topics. <u>Unfocused, even disorganized</u> paragraphs result when that happens.

2. **Analyze**
   a. Are the underlined words a relatively small set of related ideas? Even if *you* see how they are related, will your readers? For that passage, the answer is no.
   b. Do the underlined words name the most important characters, real or abstract? Again, the answer is no.

3. **Rewrite**
   a. In most (not necessarily all) of your sentences, use subjects to name their topics.
   b. Be sure that those topics are, in context, familiar to your readers.

Here is that passage revised, with the new topics boldfaced.

> **Readers** understand what a passage is generally about when **they** see consistent ideas toward the beginnings of sentences, especially in

their subjects. **They** feel a passage is coherent when **they** read a sequence of topics that focuses on a narrow set of related ideas. But when topics seem to shift randomly, **readers** lose the context of each sentence. When **that** happens, **they** feel they are reading paragraphs **that** are unfocused and even disorganized.

AVOIDING DISTRACTIONS AT THE BEGINNING OF A SENTENCE

It's hard to begin a sentence well. Readers want to get to topics/subjects quickly, but too often, we begin sentences in ways that keep readers from getting there. It's called *throat-clearing*. Throat-clearing typically begins with metadiscourse (review pp. 51–53) that connects a sentence to the previous one. These include common transitions such as *and, but, therefore*:

> And therefore . . .

We then add a second kind of metadiscourse that expresses our attitude toward what is coming, words such as *fortunately, perhaps, allegedly, it is important to note, for the most part*, or *politically speaking*:

> And therefore, it is important to note . . .

Then we indicate time, place, or manner:

> And therefore, it is important to note that, in eastern states since 1980 . . .

Only then do we get to the topic/subject:

> And, therefore, it is important to note that, in eastern states since 1980, **acid rain** has become a serious problem.

When you open several sentences with distractions like that, your readers have a hard time seeing not just what each sentence is about, but the focus of a whole passage. When you find a sentence with lots of words before its subject/topic, revise:

> ✓ Since 1980, therefore, **acid rain** has become a political problem in the eastern states.

> ***Here's the point:*** In most of your sentences (not necessarily all), start with the subject and make that subject the topic of the sentence.

INTEGRATING THE PRINCIPLES

We can bring together these principles about old and new and strings of consistent topics with the principles about characters as subjects and actions as verbs (I'll fill in the empty boxes in Lesson 5).

Learning to write clear sentences is hard enough. Even more demanding is assembling those sentences into a passage that is both cohesive and coherent. The nineteenth-century essayist Thomas De Quincey understood its importance:

> The two capital secrets in the art of prose composition are these: first the philosophy of translation and connection; . . . all fluent and effective composition depends on the connections; secondly, the way in which sentences are made to modify each other; for the most powerful effects in which eloquence arise out of this reverberation, as it were, from each other in a rapid succession of sentences.

5

Emphasis

In the end is my beginning.
—T. S. ELIOT

UNDERSTANDING HOW SENTENCES END

If you consistently write sentences whose subject/topics name a few central characters and join them to strong verbs, you'll likely get the rest of the sentence right, and in the process create a passage that is both cohesive and coherent. But if the first few words of a sentence are worth special attention, so are the last few, because how you end a sentence determines how readers judge both its clarity and its strength. In this lesson, we address clarity first, then strength, then how the right emphasis on the right words can contribute to coherence.

When readers build up momentum in the first nine or ten words of a sentence, they more easily get through complicated material that follows. Compare:

1a. A sociometric and actuarial analysis of Social Security revenues and disbursements for the last six decades to determine changes in projecting deficits is the subject of this study.

> ✓ 1b. In this study, we analyze Social Security's revenues and disbursements for the last six decades, using sociometric and actuarial criteria to determine changes in projecting deficits.

As we start (1a), we struggle to understand its technical terms at the same time we are hacking through a subject twenty-two words long. In (1b), we go through just five words to get past a subject and verb and twelve more before we hit a term that might slow us up. By that point we have enough momentum to carry us through the complexity to its end. In short, in (1a), we hit the complexity at the beginning; in (1b), we don't hit it until near the end, where we can handle it better.

There are, however, two sources of complexity: grammar and meaning.

Complex Grammar

Which of these two sentences do you prefer?

> 2a. Lincoln's claim that the Civil War was God's punishment of both North and South for slavery appears in the last part of the speech.
>
> 2b. In the last part of his speech, Lincoln claims that God gave the Civil War to both North and South as a punishment for slavery.

Most readers prefer (2b), because it begins simply with a short introductory phrase followed by a one-word subject and a specific verb, then moves toward grammatical complexity. We discussed that issue in Lesson 4.

Complex Meaning

Another kind of complexity is in the meanings of words, especially technical terms. Compare these two passages:

> 3a. The role of calcium blockers in the control of cardiac irregularity can be seen through an understanding of the role of calcium in the activation of muscle cells. The proteins actin, myosin, tropomyosin, and troponin make up the sarcomere, the basic unit of muscle contraction. The energy-producing, or ATPase, protein myosin makes up its thick filament, while the regulatory proteins actin, tropomyosin, and troponin make up its thin filament. Interaction of myosin and actin triggers muscle contraction.

✓ 3b. When a muscle contracts, it uses calcium. We must therefore understand how calcium affects muscle cells to understand how cardiac irregularity is controlled by the drugs called "calcium blockers." The basic unit of muscle contraction is the sarcomere. It has two filaments, one thin and one thick. Those filaments consist of four proteins that regulate contraction: actin, tropomyosin, and troponin in the thin filament and myosin in the thick one. Muscles contract when the regulatory protein actin in the thin filament interacts with myosin, an energy-producing or ATPase protein in the thick filament.

Both passages use the same technical terms, but (3b) is clearer to those who know nothing about the chemistry of muscles.

Those passages differ in two ways. First, information that is only implicit in (3a) is explicit in (3b):

3a. . . . and troponin make up the sarcomere, the basic unit of muscle contraction. The energy-producing, or ATPase, protein myosin, makes up its thick filament . . . .

3b. The basic unit of muscle contraction is the sarcomere. It has two filaments, one thin and one thick.

More important, note how almost all the technical terms in (3a) are toward the beginnings of their sentences and the familiar ones are toward the end:

3a. The role of **calcium blockers** in the control of **cardiac irregularity** can be seen through an understanding of the role of calcium in the activation of muscle cells.

The proteins actin, myosin, tropomyosin, and troponin make up the **sarcomere,** the basic unit of muscle contraction.

The energy-producing, or ATPase, protein myosin makes up its thick filament,

while **the regulatory proteins** actin, tropomyosin, and troponin make up its thin filament.

Interaction of myosin and actin triggers muscle contraction.

In (3b), I moved those technical terms to the ends of their sentences:

. . . uses **calcium.**

. . . controlled by the drugs called " **calcium blockers."**

. . . is the **sarcomere.**

. . . four proteins that regulate contraction: **actin, tropomyosin,** and **troponin** in the thin filament and **myosin** in the thick one.

. . ., an **energy-producing or ATPase protein** in the thick filament.

These principles work for prose intended even for professional readers. In this next passage from the *New England Journal of Medicine,* the writer deliberately uses metadiscourse just to put a new technical term at the end:

> The incubation of peripheral-blood lymphocytes with a lymphokine, interleukin-2, generates lymphoid cells that can lyse fresh, noncultured, natural-killer-cell-resistant tumor cells but not normal cells. *We term these cells* **lymphokine-activated killer (LAK) cells.**

Here's the point: Your readers want you to use the end of your sentences to help them manage two kinds of difficulty:

- long and complex phrases and clauses
- new information, particularly unfamiliar technical terms

In general, begin sentences with elements that are relatively short: a short introductory phrase or clause, followed by a short, concrete subject, followed by a verb expressing a specific action. After the verb, the sentence can go on for several lines, if it is well constructed (see Lesson 7). The general principle is to carry the reader from simplicity to complexity. We can integrate that principle with our others:

Fixed		
Variable	Familiar, simple, short	
Fixed	Subject	Verb	—
Variable	Character	Action	

ONE MORE NEW TERM: *STRESS*

In the last lesson, we said that an important position in the *psychological* geography of a sentence is its first few words, because they name the topic of a sentence, its *psychological* as opposed to its grammatical subject (see pp. 41–42). So far in this lesson, I've discussed the end of a sentence in general, but its last few words are particularly important. You can sense that when you hear your voice rise at the end of sentence to emphasize one syllable more strongly than the others:

. . . more strongly than the ^{6}-thers.

We have the same experience when reading silently.

We'll call this most emphatic part of a sentence its *stress* and add it to our last box. How you manage the emphasis in that stress position helps establish the voice readers hear in your prose, because if you end a sentence on light words that carry little meaning, your sentence will seem to end weakly.

Global warming could raise sea levels to a point where much of the world's low-lying coastal areas would disappear, **according to most atmospheric scientists.**

✓ According to most atmospheric scientists, global warming could raise sea levels to a point where much of the world's low-lying coastal areas **would disappear.**

Fixed	Topic	
Variable	Familiar, short, simple	New, complex, long
Fixed	Subject	Verb	——
Variable	Character	Action	——

In Lesson 3, we saw how different subject/topics create different points of view (pp. 29–30). You can also create different stylistic effects by managing how your sentences end.

Compare these next passages. One was written to blame an American president for being weak with Iran on arms control. The other is a revision that stresses Iran. The ends of the sentences tell you which is which:

1a. The administration has blurred an issue central to nuclear arms control, **the issue of verification**. Irresponsible charges, innuendo, and leaks have submerged **serious problems with Iranian compliance**. The objective, instead, should be not to exploit these concerns in order to further poison our relations, repudiate existing agreements, or, worse still, terminate arms control altogether, but to **insist on compliance and clarify questionable behavior**.

1b. The issue of verification—so central to arms control—has been **blurred by the administration**. Serious problems with Iranian compliance have been submerged in **irresponsible charges, innuendo, and leaks**. The objective, instead, should be to clarify questionable behavior and insist on compliance—not to exploit these concerns in order to **further poison our relations, repudiate existing agreements, or, worse still, terminate arms control altogether.**

Here's the point: Just as we look to the first few words for point of view, we look to the last few words for special emphasis. You can revise a sentence to emphasize particular words that you want readers to hear stressed and thereby note as particularly significant.

DIAGNOSIS AND REVISION: STRESS

If you have managed your subjects and topics well, you will by default put the words you want to emphasize toward the ends of your sentences. To test this, read your sentence aloud, and as you reach the last three or four words, tap your finger hard as if emphasizing them in a speech. If you tap on words that do not deserve strong emphasis, look for words that do, then put those words closer to the end. Here are some ways to do that.

Three Tactical Revisions

1. Trim the end.

Sociobiologists claim that our genes control our social behavior **in the way we act in situations we are in every day.**

Since *social behavior* means *the way we act in situations ...*, we drop everything after *behavior:*

✓ Sociobiologists claim that our genes **control our social behavior.**

2. Shift peripheral ideas to the left.

The data offered to prove ESP are weak, **for the most part.**

✓ **For the most part,** the data offered to prove ESP are **weak.**

Particularly avoid ending with anticlimactic metadiscourse:

Job opportunities in computer programming are getting scarcer, **it must be remembered.**

✓ **It must be remembered** that job opportunities in computer programming are getting scarcer.

3. Shift new information to the right.

A more common way to manage stress is by moving new information to the end of a sentence.

Questions about the ethics of withdrawing intravenous feeding are *more difficult [than something just mentioned].*

✓ *More difficult [than something just mentioned]* are **questions about the ethics of withdrawing intravenous feeding.**

Six Syntactic Devices to Emphasize the Right Words

There are several syntactic devices that let you manage where in a sentence you stress units of new information. You just read one of them.

1. ***There*** Some editors discourage all *there is/there are* constructions, but a *there* lets you shift a subject to the right, thereby emphasizing it. Compare:

Several syntactic devices let you manage where in a sentence you locate units of new information.

✓ *There are* **several syntactic devices** that let you manage where in a sentence you locate units of new information.

Experienced writers commonly begin a paragraph with *there* to introduce new topics and concepts that they develop in what follows.

2. **Passives (for the last time)** A passive verb lets you flip a subject and object. Compare these next two sentences:

> Some claim that **our genes** influence$_{active}$ aspects of behavior that we think are learned. **Our genes,** for example, seem to determine . . .

> ✓ Some claim that aspects of behavior that we think are learned are in fact influenced$_{passive}$ **by our genes. Our genes,** for example, seem to determine . . .

The passive is in the language so that we can get old and new information in the right order.

3. ***What* shift** This is another device that shifts a part of the sentence to the right, thereby emphasizing it more:

> We need a monetary policy that would end fluctuations in money supply, unemployment, and inflation.

> ✓ **What** we need **is** a monetary policy that would end fluctuations in money supply, unemployment, and inflation.

4. ***It* shift** When you have a subject consisting of a long noun clause, you can move it to the end of the sentence and start with an *it*:

> **That oil prices would be set by OPEC** once seemed inevitable.

> ✓ *It* once seemed inevitable **that oil prices would be set by OPEC.**

5. ***Not only X, but Y (as well)*** In this next pair, note how the *but* emphasizes the last element of the pair:

> We must clarify these issues **and develop deeper trust.**

> ✓ We must *not only* clarify these issues, *but* **develop deeper trust.**

Unless you have reason to emphasize the negative, end with the positive:

> The point is to highlight our success, **not to emphasize our failures.**

> ✓ The point is not to emphasize our failures, but **to highlight our success.**

6. **Pronoun substitution, and ellipsis** This is a fine point: a sentence can end flatly when you repeat a word that you used just a few words before at the end of a sentence, because the voice we hear in our mind's ear drops off at the end. If you read aloud the preceding sentence, this one, and the next, you can hear that drop at the end of each sentence. To avoid that kind of flatness, rewrite or use a pronoun instead of repeating the word at the end of the sentence. For example:

> A sentence will seem to end flatly if at its end you use a word that you used just a few words before, because when you repeat that word, your voice **drops.** Instead of repeating the noun, use a **pronoun.** The reader will at least hear emphasis on the word just **before** *it.*

Occasionally, you can just delete words that repeat earlier ones:

> It is sometimes possible to represent a complex idea in a simple sentence, but more often you cannot.

One of the characteristics of especially elegant prose is how writers use a handful of rhetorical figures to end their sentences. I will discuss those devices in Lesson 8.

Topics, Emphasis, Themes, and Coherence

There is one more function performed by the stress of certain sentences, one that helps readers think a whole passage is coherent. As we saw in the last lesson, readers take the clearest topic to be a short noun phrase that comes early in a sentence, usually as its subject. That's why most of us judge this next paragraph to be unfocused: its sentences seem to open randomly, from no consistent point of view:

> 1a. Great strides in the early and accurate diagnosis of Alzheimer's disease have been made in recent years. Not too long ago, senility in an older patient who seemed to be losing touch with reality was often confused with Alzheimer's. Genetic clues have become the basis of newer and more reliable tests in the last few years, however. The risk of human tragedy of another kind, though, has resulted from the

increasing accuracy of these tests: predictions about susceptibility to Alzheimer's have become possible long before the appearance of any overt symptoms. At that point, an apparently healthy person could be devastated by such an early diagnosis.

If we revise that passage to make the topics more consistent, we also make it more coherent (topics are boldfaced):

> ✓ 1b. In recent years, **researchers** have made great strides in the early and accurate diagnosis of Alzheimer's disease. Not too long ago, when a **physician** examined an older patient who seemed out of touch with reality, **she had** to guess whether the **person** was senile or had Alzheimer's. In the past few years, however, **physicians** have been able to use new and more reliable tests focusing on genetic clues. But in **the accuracy of these new tests** lies the risk of another kind of human tragedy: **physicians** may be able to predict Alzheimer's long before its overt appearance, but **such an early diagnosis** could psychologically devastate an apparently healthy person.

The passage now focuses on just two topics: researchers/physicians and testing/diagnosis.

But there is one more revision that would make that passage even more of a whole:

> Put key words in the stress position of the *first* sentence of a passage to emphasize the ideas that organize the rest of it.

The first sentence of that paragraph stresses advances in diagnosis: . . . *the early and accurate diagnosis of Alzheimer's disease.* But the point in this passage is not about diagnosis, but about its risks. That organizing concept does not, however, appear until we are more than halfway through that paragraph.

Readers would grasp the point of that passage better if all of its key concepts appeared in the first sentence, *specifically toward its end, in its stress position.* Readers read the opening sentence or two of a paragraph to find the key concepts that the paragraph will repeat and develop, *and they specifically look for those concepts in the last few words of those opening, introductory, framing sentences.*

Here is a new first sentence for the Alzheimer's paragraph that would help readers focus on the key concepts not just of

Alzheimer's and *new diagnoses,* but of *new problem* and *informing those most at risk.*

> In recent years, researchers have made great strides in the early and accurate diagnosis of Alzheimer's disease, but those **diagnoses** have raised **a new problem** about **informing those most at risk who show no symptoms of it.**

We can call those key concepts that run through a passage its *themes.*

Look at the highlighted words in the passage below one more time:

- The boldfaced words are about testing.
- The italicized words are about mental states.
- The capitalized words are about a new problem.

Each of those concepts is announced toward the end of a new opening sentence, especially the theme of the new problem.

> ✓ 1c. In recent years, researchers have made great strides in the early and accurate **diagnosis** of *Alzheimer's disease,* but those **diagnoses** have raised A NEW PROBLEM about INFORMING THOSE *MOST AT RISK* WHO SHOW *NO SYMPTOMS OF IT.* Not too long ago, when a physician examined an older patient who seemed *out of touch with reality,* she had to **guess** whether that person had *Alzheimer's* or was *only senile.* In the past few years, however, physicians have been able to use **new and more reliable tests** focusing on genetic clues. But in the accuracy of these **new tests** lies the RISK OF ANOTHER KIND OF HUMAN TRAGEDY: physicians may be able to **predict** *Alzheimer's* long before its overt appearance, but such an early **diagnosis** could PSYCHOLOGICALLY DEVASTATE AN APPARENNTLY HEALTHY PERSON.

That passage now "hangs together" not for just one reason, but for three:

- Its topics consistently focus on physicians and diagnosis.
- Running through it are strings of words that focus on the themes of (1) tests, (2) mental conditions, and (3) a new problem.

- *And no less important, the opening sentence helps us notice those themes by emphasizing them at its end.*

This principle applies to sentences that introduce fairly long paragraphs (two- or three-sentence introductory, transitional, and other kinds of paragraphs follow different patterns). It also applies to sentences that introduce passages of any length, even to a whole document.

> ***Here's the point:***   We depend on concepts running through a passage to create a sense of its coherence. You help readers identify those concepts in two ways:
>
> - Repeat those that name characters as topics of sentences, usually as subjects.
> - Repeat others as themes elsewhere in a passage, in nouns, verbs, and adjectives (see Lesson 9).
>
> Readers are more likely to notice those themes if you emphasize them at the end of the sentence that introduces that passage.

There is an old German proverb that captures this principle quite nicely:

Beginning and end shake hands with one another.

6

Concision

To a Snail: If "compression is the first grace of style,"
you have it.
—MARIANNE MOORE

UNDERSTANDING CONCISION

You get close to clarity when you match your characters and actions to your subjects and verbs, and closer yet when you get the right characters into topics and the right words under stress. But readers may still think your prose is a long way from graceful if it's anything like this:

> In my personal opinion, it is necessary that we should not ignore the opportunity to think over each and every suggestion offered.

That writer matched characters with subjects, and actions with verbs, but in too many words: opinion is always personal, so we don't need *personal,* and since this statement is opinion, we don't need *in my opinion. Think over* and *not ignore* both mean *consider. Each and every* is redundant. A suggestion is by definition offered. In fewer words:

✓ We should consider each suggestion.

Though not elegant, that sentence at least has style's first grace—compression, or as we'll call it, *concision*. Concision, though, is only a start. You must still make your sentences shapely. In this lesson, I focus on concision; in the next, on shape.

DIAGNOSIS AND REVISION

Six Principles of Concision

When I edited that sentence about suggestions, I followed six principles:

1. Delete words that mean little or nothing.
2. Delete words that repeat the meaning of other words.
3. Delete words implied by other words.
4. Replace a phrase with a word.
5. Change negatives to affirmatives.
6. Delete useless adjectives and adverbs.

Those principles are easy to state but hard to follow, because you have to inch your way through every sentence you write, cutting here, compressing there, and that's labor intensive. Those six principles, though, can guide you in that work.

1. **Delete Meaningless Words** Some words are verbal tics that we use as unconsciously as we clear our throats:

kind of	actually	particular	really	certain	various
virtually	individual	basically	generally	given	practically

   > *Productivity* actually ***depends on*** certain ***factors that*** basically ***involve psychology more than*** any particular ***technology.***

   ✓ Productivity depends on psychology more than on technology.

2. **Delete Doubled Words** Early in the history of English, writers got into the habit of pairing a French or Latin word with a native English one, because foreign words sounded more

learned. Most paired words today are just redundant. Among the common ones:

full and complete	hope and trust	any and all
true and accurate	each and every	basic and fundamental
hope and desire	first and foremost	various and sundry

3. **Delete What Readers Can Infer** This redundancy is common but hard to identify, because it comes in so many forms.

Redundant Modifiers Often, the meaning of a word implies its modifier:

Do not try to *predict* those **future** events that will **completely** *revolutionize* society, because **past** *history* shows that it is the **final** *outcome* of minor events that **unexpectedly** *surprises* us more.

✓ Do not try to predict revolutionary events, because history shows that the outcome of minor events surprises us more.

Some common redundancies:

terrible tragedy	various different	free gift
basic fundamentals	future plans	each individual
final outcome	true facts	consensus of opinion

Redundant Categories Every word implies its general category, so you can usually cut a word that names it. Compare (the category is boldfaced):

During that *period* **of time,** the *membrane* **area** became *pink* **in color** and *shiny* **in appearance.**

✓ During that *period,* the *membrane* became *pink* and *shiny.*

In doing that, you may have to change an adjective into an adverb:

The holes must be aligned in an *accurate* **manner.**

✓ The holes must be aligned *accurately.*

Sometimes you change an adjective into a noun:

The county manages the *educational* **system** and *public recreational* **activities.**

✓ The county manages *education* and *public recreation.*

Here are some general nouns (boldfaced) often used redundantly:

large in **size**	round in **shape**	honest in **character**
unusual in **nature**	of a strange **type**	**area** of mathematics
of a bright **color**	at an early **time**	in a confused **state**

General Implications This kind of wordiness is even harder to spot, because it can be so diffuse:

> Imagine someone trying to learn the rules for playing the game of chess.

Learn implies *trying, playing the game* implies *rules*, chess is a game. So more concisely,

> Imagine learning the rules of chess.

4. **Replace a Phrase with a Word** This redundancy is especially difficult to fix, because you need a big vocabulary and the wit to use it. For example:

> As you carefully read what you have written to improve wording and catch errors of spelling and punctuation, the thing to do before anything else is to see whether you can use sequences of subjects and verbs instead of the same ideas expressed in nouns.

That is,

✓ As you edit, first replace nominalizations with clauses.

I compressed five phrases into five words:

carefully read what you have written	→	edit
the thing to do before anything else	→	first
use X instead of Y	→	replace
nouns instead of verbs	→	nominalizations
sequences of subjects and verbs	→	clauses

I can offer no principle that tells you what phrases to replace with a word, much less give you the word. I can point out only that you often can, and that you should be alert for opportunities to do so—which is to say, try.

Here are some common phrases (boldfaced) to watch for. Note that some of them let you turn a nominalization into a verb (both italicized):

We must explain **the reason for** the *delay* in the meeting.
✓ We must explain **why** the meeting is *delayed*.

Despite the fact that the data were checked, errors occurred.
✓ **Even though** the data were checked, errors occurred.

In the event that you finish early, contact this office.
✓ **If** you finish early, contact this office.

In a situation where a class closes, you may petition to get in.
✓ **When** a class closes, you may petition to get in.

I want to say a few words **concerning the matter of** money.
✓ I want to say a few words **about** money.

There is a need for more careful *inspection* of all welds.
✓ You **must** *inspect* all welds more carefully.

We **are in a position** to make you an offer.
✓ We **can** make you an offer.

It is possible that nothing will come of this.
✓ Nothing **may** come of this.

Prior to the *end* of the training, apply for your license.
✓ **Before** training *ends*, apply for your license.

We have noted a **decrease/increase in** the number of errors.
✓ We have noted *fewer/more* errors.

5. **Change Negatives to Affirmatives** When you express an idea in a negative form, not only must you use an extra word: *same* → *not different*, but you also force readers to do a kind of algebraic calculation. These two sentences, for example, mean much the same thing, but the affirmative is more direct:

Do not write in the negative. → Write in the affirmative.

You can rewrite most negatives:

not careful	→	careless	not allow	→	prevent
not many	→	few	not stop	→	continue
not the same	→	different	not notice	→	overlook
not often	→	rarely	not include	→	omit

Do not translate a negative into an affirmative if you want to emphasize the negative. (Is that such a sentence? I could have written, *Keep a negative sentence when . . . .*)

Some verbs, prepositions, and conjunctions are implicitly negative:

Verbs	*preclude, prevent, lack, fail, doubt, reject, avoid, deny, refuse, exclude, contradict, prohibit, bar*
Prepositions	*without, against, lacking, but for, except*
Conjunctions	*unless, except when*

You can baffle readers if you combine *not* with these negative words. Compare these:

> **Except** when you have **failed** to submit applications **without** documentation, benefits will **not** be **denied.**

✓ You will receive benefits only if you submit your documents.

✓ To receive benefits, submit your documents.

And you baffle readers completely when you combine explicitly and implicitly negative words with passives and nominalizations:

> There should be **no** submission of payments **without** notification of this office, **unless** the payment does **not** exceed $100.

> Do not **submit** payments if you have not **notified** this office, unless you are **paying** less than $100.

Now revise the negatives into affirmatives:

✓ If you pay more than $100, notify this office first.

6. **Delete Adjectives and Adverbs** Many writers can't resist adding useless adjectives and adverbs. Try deleting every

adverb and every adjective before a noun, then restore *only* those that readers need to understand the passage. In this passage, which ones should be restored?

> At the heart of the argument culture is our habit of seeing issues and ideas as ~~absolute and irreconcilable~~ principles ~~continually~~ at war. To move beyond this ~~static and limiting~~ view, we can remember the ~~Chinese~~ approach to yin and yang. They are two principles, yes, but they are conceived not as ~~irreconcilable polar~~ opposites but as elements that coexist and should be brought into balance ~~as much as possible~~. As sociolinguist Suzanne Wong Scollon notes, "Yin is always present in and changing into yang and vice versa." How can we translate this ~~abstract~~ idea into ~~daily~~ practice?
>
> —Deborah Tannen, *The Argument Culture*

Here's the point: Readers think you write concisely when you use only enough words to say what you mean.

1. Delete words that mean little or nothing.
2. Delete words that repeat the meaning of other words.
3. Delete words implied by other words.
4. Replace a phrase with a word.
5. Change negatives to affirmatives.
6. Delete useless adjectives and adverbs.

A Particular Kind Of Redundancy: Metadiscourse

Lesson 4 described metadiscourse as language that refers to the following:

- the writer's intentions: *to sum up, candidly, I believe*
- directions to the reader: *note that, consider now, as you see*
- the structure of the text: *first, second, finally, therefore, however*

Everything you write needs metadiscourse, but too much buries your ideas:

> The last point I would like to make is that in regard to men-women relationships, it is important to keep in mind that the greatest changes have occurred in how they work together.

Only nine of those thirty-four words address men-women relationships:

> men-women relationships . . . greatest changes . . . how they work together.

The rest is metadiscourse:

> The last point I would like to make is that in regard to . . . it is important to keep in mind that . . .

When we prune the metadiscourse, we tighten the sentence:

> The greatest changes in men-women relationships have occurred in how they work together.

Now that we see what the sentence says, we can make it still more direct:

> ✓ Men and women have changed their relationships most in how they work together.

Some teachers and editors urge us to cut all metadiscourse, but everything we write needs some. You have to read with an eye to how good writers in your field use it, then do likewise.

There are, however, some types that you can usually cut.

Metadiscourse That Attributes Your Ideas to a Source Don't announce that something has been *observed, noticed, noted,* and so on; just state the fact:

> High divorce rates **have been observed** to occur in areas that **have been determined to have** low population density.
> ✓ High divorce rates occur in areas with low population density.

Metadiscourse That Announces Your Topic The boldface phrases tell your reader what your sentence is "about":

> **This section introduces another** problem, that of noise pollution. **The first thing to say about it is** that noise pollution exists not only . . .

Readers catch the topic more easily if you reduce the metadiscourse:

> ✓ **Another** problem is noise pollution. **First,** it exists not only . . .

Two other constructions call attention to a topic, usually one already mentioned in the text:

> **In regard to** a vigorous style, the most important feature is a short, concrete subject followed by a forceful verb.
>
> **So far as** China's industrial development **is concerned,** it will take only a few years to equal that of Japan.

But you can usually work those topics into a subject:

> ✓ **The most important feature of a vigorous style** is a short, concrete subject followed by a forceful verb.
> ✓ **China** will take only a few years to equal Japan's industrial development.

Metadiscourse That Hedges and Intensifies Some metadiscourse reflects the writer's certainty about what she is claiming. This kind comes in two flavors, *hedges* and *intensifiers*. Hedges limit your certainty; intensifiers increase it. Both can influence how readers judge your character, because they signal how well you balance caution and confidence.

Hedges   These are common hedges:

Adverbs	*usually, often, sometimes, almost, virtually, possibly, allegedly, arguably, perhaps, apparently, in some ways, to a certain extent, somewhat, in some/certain respects*
Adjectives	*most, many, some, a certain number of*

Verbs	*may, might, can, could, seem, tend, appear, suggest, indicate*

Some readers think all hedging is not just redundant, but mealy-mouthed:

> There **seems to be some** evidence to **suggest** that **certain** differences between Japanese and Western rhetoric **could** derive from historical influences **possibly** traceable to Japan's cultural isolation and Europe's history of cross-cultural contacts.

On the other hand, only a fool or someone with vast historical evidence would make a claim as confident as this:

> This evidence **proves** that Japanese and Western rhetorics differ because of Japan's cultural isolation and Europe's history of cross-cultural contacts.

In most academic writing, we more often state claims closer to this (note my own hedging; compare the more assertive, *In academic writing, we state claims like this*):

> ✓ This evidence **suggests** that **aspects** of Japanese and Western rhetoric differ because of Japan's cultural isolation and Europe's history of cross-cultural contacts.

The verbs *suggest* and *indicate* let you state a claim about which you are less than 100 percent certain, but confident enough to propose:

> ✓ The evidence **indicates** that some of these questions remain unresolved.
>
> ✓ These data **suggest** that further studies are necessary.

Even confident scientists hedge. This next paragraph introduced the most significant breakthrough in the history of genetics, the discovery of the double helix of DNA. If anyone was entitled to be assertive, it was Crick and Watson. But they chose to be diffident (note, too, the first-person *we;* hedges are boldfaced):

> We **wish to suggest a** [not *the*] structure for the salt of deoxyribose nucleic acid (D.N.A.) . . . . A structure for nucleic acid has already been proposed by Pauling and Corey . . . . **In our opinion,** this structure is unsatisfactory for two reasons: (1) **We believe** that the material which

gives the X-ray diagrams is the salt, not the free acid . . . . (2) **Some** of the van der Waals distances **appear** to be too small.

—J. D. Watson and F. H. C. Crick, "Molecular Structure of Nucleic Acids"

Without the hedges, their claim would be more concise but more aggressive. Compare this (I boldface the stronger words, but most of the more aggressive tone comes from the absence of hedges):

We ~~wish to suggest~~ **state here the** structure for the salt of deoxyribose nucleic acid (D.N.A.) . . . . A structure for nucleic acid has already been proposed by Pauling and Corey . . . . ~~In our opinion~~, [T]his structure is unsatisfactory for two reasons: (1) ~~We believe that~~ [T]he material which gives the X-ray diagrams is the salt, not the free acid . . . . (2) ~~Some of~~ [T]he van der Waals distances ~~appear to be~~ **are** too small.

Intensifiers   These are common intensifiers:

Adverbs	*very, pretty, quite, rather, clearly, obviously, undoubtedly, certainly, of course, indeed, inevitably, invariably, always*
Adjectives	*key, central, crucial, basic, fundamental, major, principal, essential*
Verbs	*show, prove, establish, as you/we/everyone knows/can see, it is clear/obvious that*

The most common intensifier is the absence of a hedge. In this case, less is more. The first sentence below has no intensifiers at the blanks, but neither does it have any hedges, and so it seems like a strong claim:

_____ Americans believe that the federal government is _____ intrusive and _____ authoritarian.

✓ **Many** Americans believe that the federal government is **often** intrusive and **increasingly** authoritarian.

Confident writers use intensifiers less often than they use hedges because they want to avoid sounding as assertive as this:

For a century now, **all** liberals have argued against **any** censorship of art, and **every** court found their arguments so **completely** persuasive that **not a** person **any** longer remembers how they were countered. As a result, today, censorship is **totally** a thing of the past.

Some writers think that kind of aggressive style is persuasive. Quite the opposite: if you state a claim moderately, readers are more likely to consider it thoughtfully:

For **about** a century now, **many** liberals have argued against censorship of art, and **most** courts have found their arguments persuasive **enough** that **few** people **may** remember **exactly** how they were countered. As a result, today, censorship is **virtually** a thing of the past.

Some claim that a passage hedged that much is wordy and weak. Perhaps. But it does not come on like a bulldozer. It leaves room for a reasoned and equally moderate response.

Here's the point: You need some metadiscourse in everything you write, especially metadiscourse that guides readers through your text, words such as *first, second, therefore, on the other hand,* and so on. You also need some metadiscourse that hedges your certainty, words such as *perhaps, seems, could,* and so on. The risk is in using too many.

For the best writers, a concern with style always begins by thinking about readers. That's what motivated the founder of the Methodist church, John Wesley:

I write for those who judge of books, not by the quantity, but by the quality of them: who ask not how long, but how good they are? I spare both my reader's time and my own, by couching my sense in as few words as I can.

7

Shape

Sentences in their variety run from simplicity to complexity, a progression not necessarily reflected in length: a long sentence may be extremely simple in construction—indeed must be simple if it is to convey its sense easily.

—SIR HERBERT

UNDERSTANDING THE SHAPE OF SENTENCES

If you can write clear and concise sentences, you have achieved a good deal. But a writer who can't write a clear sentence longer than twenty words or so is like a composer who can write only jingles. Some advise against long sentences, but you cannot communicate every complex idea in a short one: you have to know how to write a sentence that is both long and clear.

Consider, for example, this sentence:

> In addition to differences in religion that have for centuries plagued Sunnis and Shiites, explanations of the causes of their distrust must include all of the other social, economic, and cultural conflicts that have plagued them that are rooted in a troubled history that extends 1,300 years into the past.

Even if that idea needed all those words (it doesn't), they could be arranged into a more shapely sentence.

We can start revising by editing the abstractions into character/subjects and action/verbs and then break the sentence into shorter ones:

> Historians have tried to explain why Sunnis and Shiites distrust one another today. Many have claimed that the sources of conflict are age-old differences in religion. But they must also consider all the other social, economic, and cultural conflicts that have plagued their 1,300 years of troubled history.

But that passage feels choppy. We prefer something like this:

> ✓ To explain why Sunnis and Shiites distrust one another today, historians must study not only age-old religious differences, but all the other social, economic, and cultural conflicts that have plagued their 1,300 years of troubled history.

That sentence is thirty-six words long, but it doesn't sprawl. So it can't be length alone that makes a sentence ungainly. In this lesson, I focus on how to write sentences that are not only long and complex but clear and shapely.

DIAGNOSIS AND REVISION: SPRAWL

As with other issues of style, you can see sprawl in the writing of others more easily than in your own, so you have to diagnose your prose in ways that sidestep your intractable subjectivity.

Start by picking out sentences longer than two lines and read them aloud. If in reading one of your long sentences you feel that you are about to run out of breath before you come to a place where you can pause to integrate all of its parts into a whole that communicates a single conceptual structure [breathe], you have found a sentence, like this one, that your readers would likely want you to revise. Or if your sentence, because of one interruption after another, seems to stop and start, your readers are, if they are typical, likely to judge that your sentence, as this one does, lurches from one part to the next.

Readers get a sense of shapeless length from three things:

- It takes readers too long to get to the verb in the main clause.
- After the verb, they have to slog through a shapeless sprawl of tacked-on subordinate clauses.
- They stumble over one interruption after another.

Revising Long Openings

Some sentences seem to take forever to get started:

> 1a. Since most undergraduate students change their fields of study at least once during their college careers, many more than once, first-year students who are not certain about their program of studies should not load up their schedules to meet requirements for a particular program.

That sentence takes thirty-one words to get to its main verb, *should not load up.* Here are two rules of thumb about beginning a sentence:

1. **Get to the subject of the main clause quickly.** Avoid beginning more than a few sentences with long introductory phrases and clauses.
2. **Get to the verb and object quickly.** Avoid long, abstract subjects and interruptions between subjects and verbs, and between verbs and their objects.

Rule of Thumb 1: Get to the Subject Quickly   We have a problem with sentences that open with long introductory phrases and clauses, because as we read them, we have to hold in mind that the subject and verb of a main clause are still to come, and that load on our memory hinders easy understanding.

Compare these next examples. In (1b), we have to read and understand seventeen words while holding in mind that we have yet to reach the main subject and verb. In (1c), we get past the subject and verb of the first clause in just three words:

> 1b. **Since most undergraduate students change their major fields of study at least once during their college careers,** *first-year students*

who are not certain about the program of studies they want to pursue SHOULD NOT LOAD UP their schedules to meet requirements for a particular program.

✓ 1c. **First-year students** SHOULD NOT LOAD UP their schedules with requirements for a particular program if they are not certain about the program of studies they want to pursue, because most CHANGE their major fields at least once during their college careers.

When you find a sentence with a very long introductory clause, try moving it to the end. If it doesn't fit there, try turning it into a sentence of its own.

It is, however, a fact of English style that clauses beginning with *if, since, when,* and *although* tend to appear before main clauses rather than after. So if you cannot avoid opening with a subordinate clause, keep it short.

An exception: In a style called "periodic" or "suspended," writers deliberately pile up introductory subordinate clauses to delay and thereby heighten the impact of a concluding main clause:

> When a society spends more on its pets than it does on its homeless,
>
> when it rewards those who hit a ball the farthest more highly than those who care most deeply for its neediest,
>
> when it takes more interest in the juvenile behavior of its richest children than in the deficient education of its poorest,
>
> it has lost its moral center.

Used sparingly, this kind of sentence can have a dramatic impact, especially when the last few words of the last clause are appropriately stressed. We discuss this matter again in Lesson 8.

Rule of Thumb 2: Get to the Verb and Object Quickly   Readers also want to get past the main subject to its verb and object. Therefore,

- Keep subjects short.
- Avoid interrupting the subject-verb connection.
- Avoid interrupting the verb-object connection.

Revise Long Subjects into Short Ones   Start by underlining whole subjects. If you find a long subject (more than seven or eight words) including nominalizations, try turning the nominalization into a verb and finding a subject for it:

> **Abco Inc.'s** *understanding* **of the drivers of its profitability in the Asian market for small electronics** helped it pursue opportunities in Africa.
>
> ✓ **Abco Inc.** was able to pursue opportunities in Africa because it understood what drove profitability in the Asian market for small electronics.

A subject can also be long if it includes a long relative clause:

> A company **that focuses on hiring the best personnel and then trains them not just for the work they are hired to do but for higher-level jobs** is likely to earn the loyalty of its employees.

Try turning the relative clause into an introductory subordinate clause beginning with *when* or *if*:

> **When a company focuses on hiring the best personnel and then trains them not just for the work they are hired to do but for higher-level jobs,** it is likely to earn the loyalty of its employees.

But if the introductory clause turns out to be as long as that one, try moving it to the end of its sentence, especially if (1) the main clause is short and to the point and (2) the moveable clause expresses newer and more complex information that supports or elaborates on the preceding main clause.

> ✓ A company is likely to earn the loyalty of its employees **when it focuses on hiring the best personnel and then trains them not just for the work they are hired to do but for higher-level jobs.**

Or better yet, perhaps, turn it into a sentence of its own.

> ✓ Some companies focus on hiring the best personnel and then train them not just for the work they are hired to do but for higher-level jobs later. **Such companies are likely to earn the loyalty of their employees.**

Avoid Interrupting the Subject-Verb Connection   You also frustrate readers when you interrupt the connection between a subject and verb, like this:

> Some scientists, **because they write in a style that is impersonal and objective,** do not easily communicate with lay people.

That *because* clause after the subject forces us to hold our mental breath until we reach the verb, *do not easily communicate.* Move the interruption to the beginning or end of its sentence, depending on whether it connects more closely to what precedes or follows it (note the *since* instead of *because*):

> ✓ Since some scientists write in a style that is impersonal and objective, they do **not easily communicate with laypeople. This lack of communication** damages . . .

> ✓ Some scientists do not easily communicate with laypeople because they write in **a style that is impersonal and objective. It is a kind of style** filled with passives and . . .

We mind short interruptions less:

> ✓ Some scientists **deliberately** write in a style that is impersonal and objective.

Avoid Interrupting the Verb-Object Connection   We also like to get past the verb to its object quickly. This sentence doesn't let us do that:

> We must develop, **if we are to become competitive with other companies in our region,** a core of knowledge regarding the state of the art in effective industrial organizations.

Move the interrupting element to the beginning or end of its sentence, depending on what comes next:

> ✓ If we are to compete with other companies in our region, we must develop a core of knowledge about the state of the art in effective industrial organizations. Such organizations provide . . .

> ✓ **We** must develop a core of knowledge about the state of the art in effective industrial organizations **if we are to compete with other companies in our region. Increasing competition** . . .

An exception: When a prepositional phrase you can move is shorter than a long object, try putting the phrase between the verb and object:

> In a long sentence, put the newest and most important information that you want your reader to remember **at its end.**

> ✓ In a long sentence, put **at its end** the newest and most important information that you want your reader to remember.

Here's the point: Readers read most easily when you quickly get them to the subject of your main clause and then past that subject to its verb and object. Avoid long introductory phrases and clauses, long subjects, and interruptions between subjects and verbs, and between verbs and objects.

ANOTHER PRINCIPLE: STARTING WITH YOUR POINT

We can add another principle, one that applies to long sentences in particular. Compare these two:

> High-deductible health plans and Health Saving Accounts into which workers and their employers make tax-deductible deposits result in workers' taking more responsibility for their health care.

> ✓ Workers take more responsibility for their health care when they adopt high-deductible insurance plans and Health Saving Accounts into which they and their employers deposit tax-deductible contributions.

Unlike that lumbering first sentence, the second follows those four principles: it begins not with a long, abstract subject but with a short, concrete one familiar to readers, directly followed by a verb stating a specific action: *Workers take . . . .*

But it differs in another way. In that first sentence, we have to read more than twenty words before we see their relevance to its key claim, to its most important *point*: that workers take responsibility for their health care. The sentence feels backward. We can't see the relevance of its beginning until we reach its end.

[High-deductible health plans and Health Saving Accounts into which workers and their employers make tax-deductible deposits]_{explanation/support} [result in workers' taking more responsibility for their health care.]_{point}

In contrast, the second sentence opens with an eight-word main clause stating its most important point clearly and concisely:

✓ [Workers take more responsibility for their health care]_{point} [when they adopt high-deductible insurance plans and Health Saving Accounts into which they and their employers make tax-deductible deposits.]_{explanation/support}

When we read its point first, we can anticipate the relevance of the next nineteen words *even before we read them.*

Here is a very general principle about how we read: we can best manage complexity when we begin with something short and direct that frames the more complex information that follows. We have seen how that principle applies to individual subjects and verbs. But it also applies to the *logical* elements of a long sentence, to its point and to its explanation or supporting information. When a point is dribbled out or delayed, we have to reconstruct it, then mentally reassemble the sentence into its logical parts. A point clearly stated up front gives us a context to understand the complexity that follows.

To diagnose a long sentence, look first for its point, the key claim that you want readers to grasp quickly. If you find it in the middle of its sentence or at its end, revise: state it in a short, simple main clause at the beginning. Then add to it the longer, more complex information that supports or explains it. (See p. 72, however, for a competing principle.)

In fact, this principle of simple-before-complex applies to even larger units:

- Begin a paragraph with a sentence (or two) expressing its point so that readers can understand what follows (see pp. 54–56).

- Begin a section of a document with a paragraph or two stating its point (see pp. 118–121).

- Do the same for a whole document: begin with an introduction that states its point and frames the rest (see pp. 106–117).

Sentence, paragraph, section, or whole—how quickly, concisely, and *helpfully* you begin determines how easily your readers understand what follows.

RESHAPING SPRAWL

When we see the point of a sentence first, we can slog through whatever sprawling mess might follow. But we will wish we didn't have to. This next sentence begins with a clearly stated point, but then sprawls through a string of four explanatory subordinate clauses:

No scientific advance is more exciting than genetic engineering,$_{point}$ which is a new way of manipulating the elemental structural units of life itself, which are the genes and chromosomes that tell our cells how to reproduce to become the parts that constitute our bodies$_{explanation}$.

Graphically, it looks like this:

No scientific advance is more exciting than genetic engineering, *[point and subject-verb core]*

  which is a new way of manipulating the elemental structural units of life itself, *[tacked-on relative clause]*

    which are the genes and chromosomes *[tacked-on relative clause]*

      that tell our cells how to reproduce to become the parts *[tacked-on relative clause]*

        that constitute our bodies. *[final tacked-on relative clause]*

Diagnose this problem by having someone read your prose aloud. If that person hesitates, stumbles over words, or runs out of breath before getting to the end of a sentence, so will your readers. You can revise in four ways.

1. Cut

Try reducing some of the relative clauses to phrases by deleting *who/that/which+is/was,* etc.:

> ✓ Of the many areas of science important to our future, few are more promising than genetic engineering, ~~which is~~ a new way of manipulating the elemental structural units of life itself, ~~which are~~ the genes and chromosomes that tell our cells how to reproduce to become the parts that constitute our bodies.

Occasionally, you have to rewrite the remaining verb into an *-ing* form:

> The day is coming when we will all have numbers **that will identify** our financial transactions so that the IRS can monitor all activities **that involve** economic activity.
>
> ✓ The day is coming when we will all have numbers ~~that will~~ **identifying** our financial transactions so that the IRS can monitor all activities ~~that~~ **involving** economic activity.

2. Turn Subordinate Clauses into Independent Sentences

> ✓ Many areas of science are important to our future, but few are more promising than genetic engineering. **It is a new way of manipulating the elemental structural units of life itself, the genes and chromosomes that tell our cells how to reproduce to become the parts that constitute our bodies.**

3. Change Clauses to Modifying Phrases

You can write a long sentence but still avoid sprawl if you change relative clauses to one of three kinds of modifying phrases: resumptive, summative, or free. You have probably never heard these terms before, but they name stylistic devices you have read many times and so should know how to use.

Resumptive Modifiers   These two examples contrast a relative clause and a resumptive modifier:

> Since mature writers often use resumptive modifiers to extend a line of thought, we need a word to name what I have not done in this

sentence, **which I could have ended after the word** *sentence* **but extended to show you a relative clause attached to a noun.**

✓ Since mature writers often use resumptive modifiers to extend a line of thought, we need a word to name what I am about to do in this sentence, **a sentence that I could have ended at that comma, but extended to show you how resumptive modifiers work.**

The boldface resumptive modifier repeats a key word, *sentence,* and rolls on.

To create a resumptive modifier, find a key noun just before the tacked-on clause, pause after it with a comma, repeat the noun, and then to that repeated word add a restrictive relative clause beginning with *that*:

> Since mature writers often use resumptive modifiers to extend a line of thought, we need a word to name what I am about to do in this sentence,
>
> a sentence
>
> **that I could have ended at that comma, but extended to show you how resumptive modifiers work.**

You can also resume with an adjective or verb. In that case, you don't add a relative clause; you just repeat the adjective or verb and continue.

✓ It was American writers who found a voice that was both **true** and **lyrical, true** to the rhythms of the working man's speech and **lyrical** in its celebration of his labor.

✓ All who value independence should **resist** the trivialization of government regulation,

   resist its obsession with administrative tidiness and compulsion to arrange things not for our convenience but for theirs.

Occasionally, you can create a resumptive modifier with the phrase *one that*:

✓ I now address a problem we have wholly ignored, **one that** has plagued societies that sell their natural resources to benefit a few today rather than using them to develop new resources that benefit everyone tomorrow.

Summative Modifiers   Here are two sentences that contrast relative clauses and summative modifiers. Notice how the *which* in the first one feels "tacked on":

> Economic changes have reduced Russian population growth to less than zero, **which will have serious social implications.**

> ✓ Economic changes have reduced Russian population growth to less than zero, **a demographic event that will have serious social implications.**

To create a summative modifier, end a grammatically complete segment of a sentence with a comma, add a term that sums up the substance of the sentence so far, and then continue with a restrictive relative clause beginning with *that*:

> Economic changes have reduced Russian population growth to less than zero,

> <u>a demographic event</u>

> **that will have serious social implications.**

A summative modifier has the same effect as a resumptive modifier: it lets you bring a clause to a sense of closure, then begin afresh.

Free Modifiers   Like the other modifiers, a free modifier can appear at the end of a clause, but instead of repeating a key word or summing up what went before, it comments on the subject of the closest verb:

> ✓ Free modifiers resemble resumptive and summative modifiers, *letting you* [i.e., the free modifier lets you] **extend the line of a sentence while avoiding a train of ungainly phrases and clauses.**

Free modifiers usually begin with an *-ing* present participle, as that one did, but they can also begin with a past participle verb, like this:

> ✓ Leonardo da Vinci was a man of powerful intellect,

> *driven* **by** [i.e., Leonardo was driven by] **an insatiable curiosity**

> and

haunted **by a vision of artistic perfection.**

A free modifier can also begin with an adjective:

✓ In 1939, we began to assist the British against Germany,
   aware [i.e., we were aware] **that we faced another world war.**

We call these modifiers *free* because they can both begin and end a sentence:

✓ **Driven by an insatiable curiosity,** Leonardo da Vinci was . . .
✓ **Aware that we faced another world war,** in 1939 we began . . .

Here's the point: When you have to write a long sentence, don't just add one phrase or clause after another, willy-nilly. Particularly avoid tacking one relative clause onto another onto another. Try extending the line of a sentence with resumptive, summative, and free modifiers.

4. Coordinate

Coordination is the real foundation of a gracefully shaped sentence. It's harder to create good coordination than good modifiers, but when done well, it's more pleasing to the reader. Compare these. My version is first; the original is second:

> The aspiring artist may find that even a minor, unfinished work which was botched may be an instructive model for how things should be done, while for the amateur spectator, such works are the daily fare which may provide good, honest nourishment, which can lead to an appreciation of deeper pleasures that are also more refined.

> ✓ For the aspiring artist, the minor, the unfinished, or even the botched work, may be an instructive model for how things should—and should not—be done. For the amateur spectator, such works are the daily fare which provide good, honest nourishment—and which can lead to appreciation of more refined, or deeper pleasures.

—Eva Hoffman, *"Minor Art Offers Special Pleasures"*

My version sprawls through a string of tacked-on clauses:

> The aspiring artist may find that even a minor, unfinished work
>> **which** was botched may be an instructive model for
>>> **how** things should be done,
>>>> **while** for the amateur spectator, such works are the daily fare
>>> **which** may provide good, honest nourishment,
>>>> **which** can lead to an appreciation of deeper pleasures
>>>>> **that** are also more refined.

Hoffman's original gets its shape from its multiple coordinations. Structurally, it looks like this:

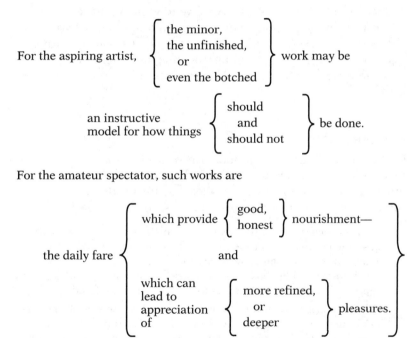

That second sentence in particular shows how elaborate coordination can get.

A General Design Principle: Short to Long

I should note one feature that distinguishes well-formed coordination. You can hear it if you read this next sentence aloud:

> We should devote a few final words to a matter that reaches beyond the techniques of research to the connections between those subjective values that reflect our deepest ethical choices and objective research.

That sentence seems to end too abruptly with *objective research*. Structurally, it looks like this:

$$
\ldots \text{between} \left\{ \begin{array}{c} \text{those subjective values that reflect our} \\ \text{deepest ethical choices} \\ \text{and} \\ \text{objective research.} \end{array} \right\}
$$

This next revision moves from shorter to longer by reversing the two coordinate elements and by adding a parallelism to the second one to make it longer still. Read this one aloud:

> ✓ We should devote a few final words to a matter that reaches beyond the techniques of research to the connections between objective research and those subjective values that reflect our deepest ethical choices and strongest intellectual commitments.

Structurally, it looks like this:

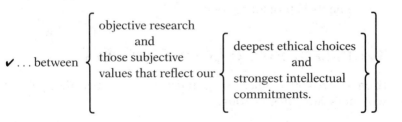

A characteristic of especially elegant prose is how its writers elaborate all these devices for extending the line of a sentence, especially balanced coordination. I will discuss those devices and their elaboration in Lesson 8.

> *Here's the point:*   Coordination lets you extend the line of a sentence more gracefully than just by tacking on one element to another. When you can coordinate, try to order the elements so that they go from shorter to longer, from simpler to more complex.

A Unifying Principle

This principle of short-to-long is, in fact, one of the unifying principles of a clear prose style:

- It applies to the subject-verb sequence of individual sentences: the shorter the better to introduce the longer, more complex elements that follow.
- It applies to the principle of old-new: old information is usually objectively shorter than new information, but it is "psychologically" shorter, as well.
- It applies to ordering the logical elements of a long sentence: begin with its short point, then add the longer and more complex information that explains or supports it.
- It applies again here in balanced coordination: put shorter elements before longer ones.

TROUBLESHOOTING LONG SENTENCES

Even when you manage their internal structures, though, long sentences can still go wrong.

Faulty Grammatical Coordination

Ordinarily, we coordinate elements only of the same grammatical structure: clause and clause, prepositional phrase and prepositional phrase, and so on. When you coordinate different grammatical structures, readers may feel you have created an offensive lack of parallelism. Careful writers avoid this:

The committee recommends {
revising the curriculum to recognize trends in local employment
and
that the division be reorganized to reflect the new curriculum.
}

They would correct that to this:

✔. . . recommends {
that the curriculum be revised to recognize . . .
and
that the division be reorganized to reflect. . . .
}

Or to this:

✔. . . recommends {
revising the curriculum to recognize . . .
and
reorganizing the division to reflect. . . .
}

However, some nonparallel coordinations do occur in well-written prose. Careful writers coordinate a noun phrase with a *how* clause:

✔ We will attempt to delineate {
the problems of education in developing nations
and
how coordinated efforts can address them in economical ways.
}

They coordinate an adverb with a prepositional phrase:

✔ The proposal appears
to have been written

quickly,
carefully,
and
with the help of many.

Careful readers do not blink at either.

Faulty Rhetorical Coordination

We respond to coordination best when the elements are coordinate not only in grammar but in thought. Some inexperienced writers coordinate by just joining one element to another with *and*:

> Grade inflation is a problem at many universities, ***and*** it leads to a devaluation of good grades earned by hard work ***and*** will not be solved simply by grading harder.

Those *and*s obscure the relationships among those claims:

> ✓ Grade inflation is a problem at many universities, **because** it devalues good grades that were earned by hard work, **but** it will not be solved simply by grading harder.

Unfortunately, I can't tell you how to recognize when elements are not coordinate in thought, except to say, "Watch for it." Which, of course, is like someone telling a batter to "hit the ball squarely." We know that. What we don't know is how.

Unclear Connections

Readers are also bothered by a coordination so long that they lose track of its internal connections and pronoun references:

> Teachers should remember that students are vulnerable and uncertain about those everyday ego-bruising moments that adults ignore and that they do not understand that one day they will become as confident and as secure as the adults that bruise them.

We sense a flicker of hesitation about where to connect:

> . . . and that they do not understand that one day they . . .

To revise a sentence like that, shorten the first half of the coordination so that you can start the second half closer to the point where the coordination began:

> ✓ Teachers should remember that students are vulnerable to ego-bruising moments that adults ignore and that they do not understand that one day . . .

If you can't do that, repeat a word that reminds the reader where the coordination began (thereby creating a resumptive modifier):

> ✓ Teachers should try to remember that students are vulnerable to ego-bruising moments that adults ignore, **to remember** that they do not understand that . . .

Ambiguous Modifiers

Another problem with modifiers is that sometimes readers are unsure what they modify:

> Overtaxing oneself in physical activity too frequently results in injury.

What happens too frequently, overtaxing or injuries? We can make its meaning unambiguous by moving *too frequently*:

> ✓ Overtaxing oneself too frequently in physical activity results in injury.
> ✓ Overtaxing oneself in physical activity results too frequently in injury.

A modifier at the end of a clause can ambiguously modify either a neighboring or a more distant phrase:

> Scientists have learned that their observations are as subjective as those in any other field **in recent years.**

We can move the modifier to a less ambiguous position:

> ✓ **In recent years,** scientists have learned that . . .
> ✓ Scientists have learned that **in recent years** their . . .

Dangling Modifiers

Another problem with a long sentence can be a dangling modifier. A modifier dangles when its implied subject differs from the explicit subject of the main clause:

> To overcome chronic poverty and lagging economic development in sub-Saharan Africa,_{dangling modifier} a commitment to health and education_{whole subject} is necessary for there to be progress in raising standards of living.

The implied subject of *overcome* is some unnamed agent, but the explicit subject of the main clause is *commitment*. To undangle the modifier, we make its implicit subject explicit:

> ✓ If **developed countries** are to overcome chronic poverty and lagging economic development in sub-Saharan Africa, a commitment to health and education is necessary . . .

Or better, make the implicit subject of the modifier the explicit subject of the clause:

> ✓ To overcome chronic poverty and lagging economic development in sub-Saharan Africa, **developed countries** must commit themselves to . . .

INTRINSIC SENSE

You can use these devices to shape a long yet clear sentence, but not even the best syntax can salvage incoherent content. This next sentence appeared in a Sunday *New York Times* travel section. The sentence before it had introduced the professional women of Amsterdam's red-light district:

> They are so unself-conscious about their profession that by day they can be seen standing naked in doorways, chatting with their neighbors in the shadow of the Oudekerstoren Church, which offers Saturday carillon concerts at 4 P.M. and a panoramic view of the city from its tower in summer.

This syntactically well-formed sentence opens with a coherent clause:

> They are so unself-conscious about their profession that by day they can be seen standing naked in doorways . . .

It continues with a free modifier:

> . . . chatting with their neighbors in the shadow of the Oudekerstoren Church . . .

then concludes with a relative clause with a balanced pair of direct objects:

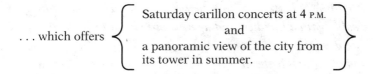

. . . which offers
- Saturday carillon concerts at 4 P.M.
  and
- a panoramic view of the city from its tower in summer.

But the movement of ideas is goofy (or evidence of a sly sense of humor). It fails a principle put forward by the nineteenth-century philosopher John Stuart Mill:

> The structure of every sentence is a lesson in logic.

8

Elegance

Anything is better than not to write clearly. There is nothing to be said against lucidity, and against simplicity only the possibility of dryness. This is a risk well worth taking when you reflect how much better it is to be bald than to wear a curly wig.

—SOMERSET MAUGHAM

UNDERSTANDING ELEGANCE

Anyone who can write clearly, concisely, and coherently should rejoice to have achieved so much. But while most of us prefer bald clarity to the density of institutional prose, others feel that relentless simplicity can be dry, even arid. It has the spartan virtue of unsalted meat and potatoes, but such fare is rarely memorable. A flash of elegance can not only fix a thought in our minds, but give us a flicker of pleasure every time we recall it. Unfortunately, I can't tell you how to do that. In fact, I incline toward those who think that the most elegant elegance is disarming simplicity.

Nevertheless, there are a few devices that can shape a thought in ways that are both elegant and clear. Just knowing them, however, is about as useful as just knowing the ingredients in a delicious bouillabaisse, then thinking you can make it. Knowing ingredients and knowing how to use them are as different as reading cookbooks and cooking. Maybe elegant clarity is a gift. But even a gift has to be educated and exercised.

Balance and Symmetry

What most makes a sentence graceful is a balance and symmetry among its parts, one echoing another in sound, rhythm, structure, and meaning. A skilled writer can balance almost any parts of a sentence, but the most common balance is based on coordination.

Balanced Coordination   Here is a balanced passage and my revision of it. A tin ear can distinguish which is which:

> The national unity of a free people depends upon a sufficiently even balance of political power to make it impracticable for the administration to be arbitrary and for the opposition to be revolutionary and irreconcilable. Where that balance no longer exists, democracy perishes. For unless all the citizens of a state are forced by circumstances to compromise, unless they feel that they can affect policy but that no one can wholly dominate it, unless by habit and necessity they have to give and take, freedom cannot be maintained.
>
> —Walter Lippmann

> The national unity of a free people depends upon a sufficiently even balance of political power to make it impracticable for an administration to be arbitrary against a revolutionary opposition that is irreconcilably opposed to it. Where that balance no longer exists, democracy perishes, because unless all the citizens of a state are habitually forced by necessary circumstances to compromise in a way that lets them affect policy with no one dominating it, freedom cannot be maintained.

My sentences lurch from one part to the next. In Lippmann's, we hear one clause and phrase echo another in word order, sound, and meaning, giving the whole passage an intricate architectural symmetry.

If we extend the idea of topic and stress from a whole sentence to its parts, we can see how he balances even short segments. Note how each significant word in one phrase echoes another in its corresponding one (I boldface topics of phrases and italicize stresses):

> The national unity of a free people depends upon a sufficiently even balance of political power to make it impracticable,

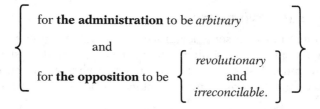

Lippmann balances the phrasal topics of *administration* and *opposition,* and closes by balancing the stressed sounds and meanings of *arbitrary, revolutionary,* and *irreconcilable.* He follows with a short concluding sentence whose stressed words are not coordinated, but still balanced (I use square brackets to indicate noncoordinated balance):

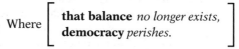

Then he creates an especially intricate design, balancing many sounds and meanings:

- He repeats *citizens* as the subject/topic of each clause: *all the citizens, they, they* (note the passive in the first one: *citizens are forced;* the active version would have unbalanced the coordination).

- He balances the sound and sense of *force* against *feel,* and the meaning of *affect policy* against the meaning of *dominate it.*

- In the last *unless* clause, he balances the meaning of *habit* against *necessity,* and the stressed *give* against *take.*

- He balances the meanings of *compromise, affect, dominate,* and *give and take.*

- Then to balance the clauses of that short preceding sentence, *balance no longer exists—democracy perishes,* he concludes with an equally short clause, *freedom cannot be maintained,* whose meaning and structure echo the corresponding pair in the preceding sentence:

balance	no longer exists
democracy	perishes
freedom	cannot be maintained

For those who notice and care, it is an impressive construction.

Uncoordinated Balance We can also balance structures that are not grammatically coordinate. In this example, the subject balances the object:

> **Scientists** whose research *creates revolutionary views of*
>   *the universe*
>   invariably upset
> **those of us** who
>
>   *construct our vision of reality*
>   *out of our common-sense experience*
>   *of it.*

Here, the predicate (everything after the subject) of a relative clause in a subject balances the predicate of the sentence:

A government
- that is unwilling to *listen* to the *moderate hopes* of *its citizenry*
- must eventually *answer* to the *harsh justice* of *its revolutionaries.*

Here, a direct object balances the object of a preposition:

Those of us concerned with our school systems will not sacrifice

- the *intellectual growth* of   our *innocent children*
- to
- the *social engineering* of   *incompetent bureaucrats.*

A more complicated balance:

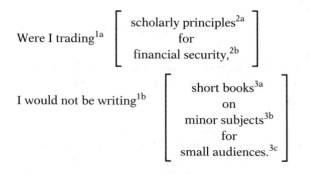

In that sentence,

- A subordinate clause (**1A**), *Were I trading,* balances the main clause (**1B**), *I would not be writing.*
- The object of that subordinate clause (**2A**), *scholarly principles,* balances the object in the prepositional phrase (**2B**), *financial security.*

- The object in the main clause (**3A**), *short books,* balances objects in two prepositional phrases, (**1B**), *minor subjects,* and (**3C**), *small audiences* (with the balanced *short, minor,* and *small*).

Remember that you usually create the most rhythmical balance when each succeeding balanced element is a bit longer than the previous one.

These patterns encourage you to think in ways that you otherwise might not. In that sense, they don't just shape your thinking; they generate it. Suppose you begin a sentence like this:

> In his earliest years, Picasso was a master draftsman of the traditional human form.

Now try this:

> In his earliest years, Picasso was **not only** a master draftsman of the traditional human form, **but also** . . .

Now you have to wonder what else he might have been. Or not have been.

I should cite another device that often appears in an elegant prose, one described in Lesson 7—resumptive and summative modifiers:

> The British Empire brought its version of administrative bureaucratic order to societies around the globe, **an order that would endure in those lands long after Britons retreated to their own shores.**

> When the poem *Howl* first appeared, the "Beats" and other avant-gardes celebrated it as a revolutionary critique of the postwar American world, **a view not shared by most mainstream literary critics, who considered it an incoherent rant.**

Here's the point: The most striking feature of elegant prose is balanced sentence structures. You most easily balance one part of a sentence against another by coordinating them with *and, or, nor, but,* and *yet,* but you can also balance noncoordinated phrases and clauses. Used to excess, these patterns can seem merely clever, but used prudently, they can emphasize an important point or conclude a line of reasoning with a flourish that careful readers notice.

CLIMACTIC EMPHASIS

How you begin a sentence determines its clarity; how you end it determines its rhythm and grace.

1. Weighty Words

When we get close to the end of a sentence, we expect words that deserve stress, so we may feel a sentence is anticlimactic if it ends on words of slight grammatical or semantic weight. At the end of a sentence, prepositions feel light—one reason we sometimes avoid leaving one there. The rhythm of a sentence should carry readers toward strength. Compare:

> Studies into intellectual differences among races is a project that only the most politically naive psychologist is willing to give support to.

> ✓ Studies into intellectual differences among races is a project that only the most politically naive scientist is willing to support.

Adjectives and adverbs are heavier than prepositions, but lighter than verbs or nouns, the heaviest of which are nominalizations. Readers have problems with nominalizations in the subject of a sentence, but at the end they provide a satisfyingly climactic thump, particularly when two of them are in coordinate balance. Consider this excerpt from Winston Churchill's "Finest Hour" speech. Churchill ended it with a parallelism climaxed by a balanced pair of nouns:

> . . . until in God's good time,

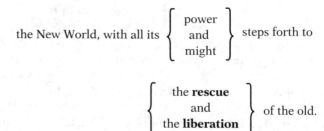

He could have written more simply, and more banally:

> ... until the New World rescues us.

2. *Of* + Weighty Word

This seems unlikely, but it's true. Look at how Churchill ends his sentence: The light *of* (followed by a lighter *a* or *the*) quickens the rhythm of a sentence just before the stress of the climactic mono-syllable, *old*:

> ... the rescue and the liberation of the **old.**

We associate this pattern with self-conscious elegance, as in the first few sentences of Edward Gibbon's *History of the Decline and Fall of the Roman Empire* (contrast that title with *History of the Roman Empire's Decline and Fall*):

> ✓ In the second century of the Christian era, the Empire of Rome comprehended **the fairest part *of* the earth,** AND **the most civilized portion *of* mankind.** The frontiers of that extensive monarchy were guarded **by ancient renown** AND **disciplined valour.** The gentle but powerful influence of laws and manners had gradually cemented **the union *of* the provinces.** Their peaceful inhabitants **enjoyed** AND **abused the advantages *of* wealth** AND **luxury.** The image of a free constitution was preserved with decent **reverence:** the Roman senate appeared to possess the sovereign authority, and devolved on the emperors all **the executive powers *of* government.**

In comparison, this is flat:

> In the second century AD, the Roman Empire comprehended **the earth's fairest, most civilized part.** Ancient renown and disciplined valour guarded **its extensive frontiers.** The gentle but powerful influence of laws and manners had gradually **unified the provinces.** Their peaceful inhabitants enjoyed and abused luxurious wealth while decently preserving what seemed to be **a free constitution.** Appearing to possess the sovereign authority, the Roman senate devolved on the emperors all **executive governmental powers.**

3. Echoing Salience

At the end of a sentence, readers hear special emphasis when a stressed word or phrase balances the sound or meaning of an earlier one. (These examples are all from Peter Gay's *Style in History.*)

> ✓ I have written these essays to anatomize this familiar yet really strange being, **style the centaur;** the book may be read as an extended critical commentary on Buffon's famous saying that **the style is the man.**

When we hear a stressed word echo an earlier one, these balances become even more emphatic:

> ✓ Apart from a few mechanical tricks of rhetoric, **manner** is indissolubly linked to **matter; style shapes,** and in turn is **shaped** by, **substance.**

> ✓ It seems frivolous, almost inappropriate, to be **stylish** about **style.**

Gay echoes both the sound and meaning of *manner* in *matter, style* in *substance, shapes* in *shaped by,* and *stylish* in *style.*

4. Chiasmus

This device (pronounced kye-**AZZ**-muss) is interesting perhaps only to those fascinated with the most arcane figures of style. The word *chiasmus* is from the Greek word for "crossing." It balances elements in two parts of a sentence, but the second part reverses the order of the elements in the first part. For example, this next sentence would be both coordinate and parallel, but it does not end with a chiasmus, because the elements in the two parts are in the same order (1A1B : 2A2B):

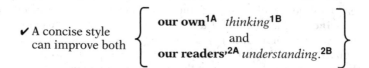

> ✔ A concise style can improve both
> $\left\{ \begin{array}{l} \textbf{our own}^{1A} \ \textit{thinking}^{1B} \\ \text{and} \\ \textbf{our readers'}^{2A} \ \textit{understanding.}^{2B} \end{array} \right.$

Were we seeking a special effect, we could reverse the order of elements in the second part to mirror those in the first. Now the pattern is not 1A1B : 2A2B, but rather 1A1B : 2B2A:

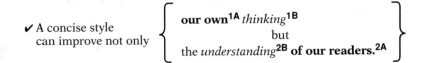

The next example is more complex. The first two elements are parallel, but the last three mirror one another: AB CDE : AB EDC:

$$
\begin{bmatrix}
\text{You}^{\textbf{A}} & \text{reveal}^{\textbf{B}} & \textbf{your own}^{\textbf{C}} & \textit{highest rhetorical}^{\textbf{D}} & \textsc{skill}^{\textbf{E}} \\
 & & \text{by the way} \\
\text{you}^{\textbf{A}} & \text{respect}^{\textbf{B}} & \textsc{the beliefs}^{\textbf{E}} & \textit{most deeply held}^{\textbf{D}} & \textbf{by your reader.}^{\textbf{C}}
\end{bmatrix}
$$

5. Suspension

Finally, you can wind up a sentence with a dramatic climax by ignoring some earlier advice. In Lesson 7, I advised you to open a sentence with its point. But self-consciously elegant writers often open a sentence with a series of parallel and coordinated phrases and clauses just so that they can delay and thereby heighten a sense of climax:

> If [journalists] held themselves as responsible for the rise of public cynicism as they hold "venal" politicians and the "selfish" public; if they considered that the license they have to criticize and defame comes with an implied responsibility to serve the public—if they did all or any of these things, they would make journalism more useful, public life, stronger, and themselves far more worthy of esteem.
>
> —James Fallows, *Breaking the News*

That sentence (the last one in Fallows's book) ends with a triple coordination. He ends it on its longest member, one that itself ends with an *of* + nominalization (*worthy of esteem*). Like all such devices, however, the impact of a long suspension is inversely proportional to its frequency; i.e., the less it's used, the bigger its bang.

> ***Here's the point:*** An elegant sentence should end on strength. You can create that strength in five ways:
>
> 1. End with a strong word, or better, a pair of them.
> 2. End with a prepositional phrase introduced by *of*.
> 3. End with an echoing salience.
> 4. End with a chiasmus.
> 5. Delay the point of the sentence with a series of suspended clauses.

EXTRAVAGANT ELEGANCE

When writers combine all these elements in a single sentence, we know they are aiming at something special, as in this next passage:

> Far from being locked inside our own skins, inside the "dungeons" of ourselves, we are now able to recognize that our minds belong, quite naturally, to a collective "mind," a mind in which we share everything that is mental, most obviously language itself, and that the old boundary of the skin is not boundary at all but a membrane connecting the inner and outer experience of existence. Our intelligence, our wit, our cleverness, our unique personalities—all are simultaneously "our own" possessions and the world's.
>
> —Joyce Carol Oates, "New Heaven and New Earth"

Here is the anatomy of that passage:

Far from being locked **inside** our own skins,

        inside the "dungeons" of ourselves,

we are now able to recognize

  that our minds belong, quite naturally, to a collective **"mind,"**

       a mind in which we share { everything that is *mental*, most obviously *language itself,*

       and

  that the old boundary of the skin is { not *boundary* at all but *a membrane* connecting the inner and outer **experience of existence.**

Our intelligence, our wit, our cleverness, our unique personalities } —all are simultaneously { "our own" possessions and the world's.

In addition to all the coordination, note the two resumptive modifiers:

  Far from being locked **inside** our own skins,

        inside the "dungeons" of ourselves . . .

  our minds belong . . . to a collective **"mind,"**

        a mind in which we share . . .

Note as well the two nominalizations stressed at the end of the first sentence and the coordinate nominalizations at the end of the second:

> . . . the inner and outer experience of existence.

> . . . "our own" possessions and the world's.

But such patterns can be more elaborate yet. Here is the last sentence from Frederick Jackson Turner's *The Frontier in American History*:

> This then is the heritage of the pioneer experience—a passionate belief that a democracy was possible which should leave the individual a part to play in a free society and not make him a cog in a machine operated from above; which trusted in the common man, in his tolerance, his ability to adjust differences with good humor, and to work out an American type from the contributions of all nations—a type for which he would fight against those who challenged it in arms, and for which in time of war he would make sacrifices, even the temporary sacrifice of his individual freedom and his life, lest that freedom be lost forever.

Note the following:

- the summative modifier in the opening segment: *a passionate belief that . . .*

- the increased length and weight of the second element in each coordination, even the coordinations inside coordinations

- the two resumptive modifiers beginning with *type* and *sacrifice*

That may be over the top, especially the quadruple chiasmus in the last sixteen words:

the temporary[1] <u>sacrifice</u>[2]   of his individual FREEDOM[3] and   *his life,*[4]
lest[4]   that FREEDOM[3]   be <u>lost</u>[2] **forever.**[1]

The meaning of *temporary* balances *forever; sacrifice* balances *lost; freedom* echoes *freedom;* and the sound of *life* balances *lest* (not to mention the near rhyme of *lest* in *lost*). You just don't see that kind of sentence anymore.

Here is the anatomy of that sentence:

This then is the heritage of the pioneer experience—
[summative modifier]   a passionate belief that a democracy was possible

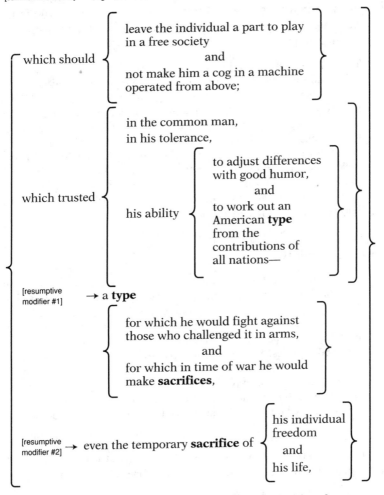

which should
- leave the individual a part to play in a free society
  and
- not make him a cog in a machine operated from above;

which trusted
- in the common man,
- in his tolerance,
- his ability
  - to adjust differences with good humor,
    and
  - to work out an American **type** from the contributions of all nations—

[resumptive modifier #1] → a **type**
- for which he would fight against those who challenged it in arms,
  and
- for which in time of war he would make **sacrifices,**

[resumptive modifier #2] → even the temporary **sacrifice** of
- his individual freedom
  and
- his life,

lest that freedom be lost forever.

Nuances of Length and Rhythm

Most writers don't plan the length of their sentences, but that's not a problem, unless every sentence is shorter than fifteen or so words, or much longer. Artful writers, however, do use the length of a sentence for a purpose. Some write short sentences to strike a note of urgency:

> Toward noon Petrograd again became the field of military action; rifles and machine guns rang out everywhere. It was not easy to tell who was shooting or where. One thing was clear; the past and the future were exchanging shots. There was much casual firing; young boys were shooting off revolvers unexpectedly acquired. The arsenal was wrecked . . . . Shots rang out on both sides. But the board fence stood in the way, dividing the soldiers from the revolution. The attackers decided to break down the fence. They broke down part of it and set fire to the rest. About twenty barracks came into view. The bicyclists were concentrated in two or three of them. The empty barracks were set fire to at once.
>
> —Leon Trotsky, *The Russian Revolution,* trans. Max Eastman

Or terse certainty:

> The teacher or lecturer is a danger. He very seldom recognizes his nature or his position. The lecturer is a man who must talk for an hour. France may possibly have acquired the intellectual leadership of Europe when their academic period was cut down to 40 minutes. I also have lectured. The lecturer's first problem is to have enough words to fill 40 or 60 minutes. The professor is paid for his time, his results are almost impossible to estimate . . . . No teacher has ever failed from ignorance. That is empiric professional knowledge. Teachers fail because they cannot "handle the class." Real education must ultimately be limited to men who INSIST on knowing, the rest is mere sheep-herding.
>
> —Ezra Pound, *ABC of Reading*

Or passion. Here, D. H. Lawrence breaks what could have been a long paragraph and long sentences into fragmented outbursts.

> Let us look at this American artist first. How did he ever get to America, to start with? Why isn't he a European still, like his father before him?

Now listen to me, don't listen to him. He'll tell you the lie you expect. Which is partly your fault for expecting it.

He didn't come in search of freedom of worship. England had more freedom of worship in the year 1700 than America had. Won by Englishmen who wanted freedom and so stopped at home and fought for it. And got it. Freedom of worship? Read the history of New England during the first century of its existence.

Freedom anyhow? The land of the free! This the land of the free! Why, if I say anything that displeases them, the free mob will lynch me, and that's my freedom. Free? Why I have never been in any country where the individual has such an abject fear of his fellow countrymen. Because, as I say, they are free to lynch him the moment he shows he is not one of them. . . .

All right then, what did they come for? For lots of reasons. Perhaps least of all in search of freedom of any sort: positive freedom, that is.

—D. H. Lawrence, *Studies in Classic American Literature*

Self-conscious stylists also write extravagantly long sentences. Here is just a piece of one whose sinuous length seems to mirror the confused progress of a protest march:

In any event, up at the front of this March, in the first line, back of that hollow square of monitors, Mailer and Lowell walked in this barrage of cameras, helicopters, TV cars, monitors, loudspeakers, and wavering buckling twisting line of notables, arms linked (line twisting so much that at times the movement was in file, one arm locked ahead, one behind, then the line would undulate about and the other arm would be ahead) speeding up a few steps, slowing down while a great happiness came back into the day as if finally one stood under some mythical arch in the great vault of history, helicopters buzzing about, chop-chop, and the sense of America divided on this day now liberated some undiscovered patriotism in Mailer so that he felt a sharp searing love for his country in this moment and on this day, crossing some divide in his own mind wider than the Potomac, a love so lacerated he felt as if a marriage were being torn and children lost—never does one love so much as then, obviously, then—and an odor of wood smoke, from where you knew not, was also in the air, a smoke of dignity and some calm heroism, not unlike the sense of freedom which also comes when a marriage is burst—Mailer knew for the first time why men in the front line of battle are almost always ready to die; there is a promise of some swift transit . . . [it goes on]

—Norman Mailer, *The Armies of the Night*

We almost feel we are eavesdropping on Mailer's stream of thought. But of course, such a sentence is the product not of an overflow of feeling but of premeditated art.

- Mailer opens with short, staccato phrases to suggest confusion, but he controls them by coordination.

- He continues the sentence by coordinating free modifiers: *arms linked . . . (line twisting . . .) speeding up . . . .*

- After several more free modifiers, he continues with a resumptive modifier: *a love so lacerated . . . .*

- After another grammatical sentence, he adds another resumptive modifier: *a smoke of dignity and some calm heroism . . . .*

> ***Here's the point***:   You need to monitor the length of your sentences only if most are longer than thirty words or shorter than fifteen. Your sentences will vary naturally if you edit them in the ways you've seen here. But if the occasion allows, don't be reluctant to experiment.

You won't acquire an elegant style just by reading this book. You must read those who write elegantly until their style runs along your muscles and nerves. Only then can you look at your own prose and know when it is elegant or just inflated. To that end, you might keep in mind George Bernard Shaw's advice to young writers:

In literature the ambition of the novice is to acquire the literary language; the struggle of the adept is to get rid of it.

Lesson

9

Global Coherence

Well begun is half done.
—ANONYMOUS

A problem well-put is half solved.
—JOHN DEWEY

UNDERSTANDING HOW FRAMEWORKS SHAPE READING

If we are deeply engaged in a topic, we will read anything about it we can get our hands on, even if we must work hard to understand it. Not only will we struggle through clotted sentences, but we'll use our prior knowledge to fill in gaps, correct lapses in logic, and make sense of a tangled organization. A writer with that kind of reader has a big advantage.

But most writers are not so lucky. Most writers face readers who are not so deeply engaged or knowledgeable. Accordingly, they have to prepare their readers in two ways:

- They have to motivate readers so that they want to read carefully.

107

- They have to let readers know what to expect so that they can read more knowledgeably.

We read most attentively when we read not just about an interesting *topic*, but about a *problem* that is important to us—from finding a good job to knowing the origins of life. When we are motivated by a problem that we know a lot about, we engage what we read so intently that it seems more clearly written and more coherent. But like the term *clear*, the term *coherent* doesn't refer to anything we find on the page. Coherence is an experience we create for ourselves as we make our own sense out of what we read.

What we look for on the page are signals that help us know what parts of our prior knowledge to bring to the text and how we can integrate what we read with the knowledge we have. You help your readers do that by building those signals into your writing deliberately. This lesson explains how to do that.

Stating Problems in Introductions

From the moment you begin to plan a writing project, don't imagine your task as just writing about a topic, passing on information that interests *you*. See yourself as posing a problem that *your readers* want to see solved. That problem might, however, be one that your readers don't yet care or even know about. If so, you face a challenge: you must overcome their inclination to ask, *So what?* And you get just one shot at answering it, in your introduction. That's where you must motivate readers to see your problem as theirs.

For example, read this introduction (these examples are much shorter than typical ones).

> 1a. When college students go out to relax on the weekend, many now "binge," downing several alcoholic drinks quickly until they are drunk or even pass out. It is a behavior that has been spreading through colleges and universities across the country, especially at large state universities. It once was done mostly by men, but now even women binge. It has drawn the attention of parents, college administrators, and researchers.

That introduction offers only a topic: it does not motivate us to care about it. Unless a reader is already engaged in the issue, she may shrug and ask, *So what? Who cares that college students drink a lot?*

Contrast that introduction with the next one: it tells us why bingeing is not just a interesting topic but a problem that requires our attention:

> 1b. Alcohol has been a big part of college life for hundreds of years. From football weekends to fraternity parties, college students drink and often drink hard. But a new kind of drinking known as "binge" drinking is spreading through our colleges and universities. Bingers drink quickly not to be sociable but to get drunk or even to pass out. Bingeing is far from the harmless fun long associated with college life. In the last six months, it has been cited in at least six deaths, many injuries, and considerable destruction of property. It crosses the line from fun to reckless behavior that kills and injures not just drinkers but those around them. We may not be able to stop bingeing entirely, but we must try to control its worst costs by educating students in how to manage its risks.

As short as that is, (1b) has the three parts that appear in most introductions. Each part has a role in motivating a reader to read on. The parts are these:

Shared Context—Problem—Solution

Alcohol has been a big part of college life . . . drink hard. _{shared context}
But a new kind of drinking known as "binge" drinking is spreading . . . kills and injures not just drinkers but those around them. _{problem}
We may not be able to stop bingeing entirely, but we must try to control its worst costs by educating students in how to manage its risks. _{solution}

Part 1: Establishing a Shared Context Not all pieces of writing open with a shared context, but most do. We see one in (1b):

> Alcohol has been a big part of college life for hundreds of years. From football weekends to fraternity parties, college students drink and often drink hard. _{shared context} But a new kind of drinking known as "binge" . . . .

That shared context offers historical background, but it might have been a recent event, a common belief, or anything else that reminds readers of what they know, have experienced, or readily accept.

> **Event:** A recent State U survey showed that 80% of first-year students engaged in underage drinking in their first month on campus, a fact that should surprise no one. _{shared context} But what is worrisome is the spread among first-year students of a new kind of drinking known as "binge" . . . .
>
> **Belief:** Most students believe that college is a safe place to drink for those who live on or near campus. And for the most part they are right. _{shared context} But for those students who get caught up in the new trend of "binge" drinking, . . .

These forms of shared context play a specific role in motivating readers to read on: In (1b), I wanted you to accept its context as a seemingly unproblematic base for thinking about binge drinking *just so that I could then challenge it.* I set you up so that I could say, in effect, *You may think you know the whole story,* **but you don't.** That *but* signals the coming qualification:

> . . . drink and often drink hard. _{shared context} **BUT a new kind of drinking known as "binge" drinking is spreading . . .**

In other words, college drinking seems unproblematic, *but it turns out not to be.* I wanted that small surprise to motivate you to go on reading.

No opening move is more common among experienced writers: open with a seeming truth, then qualify or even reject it. You can find countless examples in newspapers, magazines, and especially professional journals. This opening context can be a sentence or two, as here; in a journal, it can be paragraphs long, where it is called a *literature review,* a survey of what researchers have said that the writer will qualify or correct.

Not every piece of writing opens with this move. Some jump to the second element of an introduction: the statement of a problem.

Part 2: Stating the Problem   If the writer opens with a shared context, she will typically introduce the problem with a *but* or *however*:

> Alcohol has been a big part of college life . . . . _{shared context} **But** a kind of drinking known as "binge" drinking is spreading through our colleges and universities. Bingers drink quickly not to be sociable but to get drunk or even to pass out. Bingeing is far from the harmless fun long associated with college life. In the last six months, it has been cited in at least six deaths, many injuries, and considerable destruction of property. It crosses the line from fun to reckless behavior that kills and injures not just drinkers but those around them. _{problem} We may not be able to . . . .

The Two Parts of a Problem   Problems are more complicated than they seem. For readers to think that something is a problem, it must have two parts:

- The first part is some *condition*, situation, or recurring event: terrorism, rising tuition, binge drinking, anything that has the potential to cause trouble.

- The second part is the *intolerable consequence* of that condition, a *cost* that readers don't want to pay.

That cost is what motivates readers. They want to eliminate or at least ameliorate it, because it makes them unhappy: the cost of terrorism is injury, death, and fear; the cost of rising tuition is more money out of our pockets. If rising tuition did not make parents and students unhappy, it would be no problem.

You can identify the cost of a problem if you imagine someone asking *So what?* after you state its condition. Answer *So what?* and you have found the cost:

> But a kind of drinking known as "binge" drinking is spreading through our colleges and universities. Bingers drink quickly not to be sociable but to get drunk or even to pass out. _{condition} *So what?* **Bingeing is far from the harmless fun long associated with college life. In the last six months, it has been cited in at least six**

deaths, many injuries, and considerable destruction of property. It crosses the line from fun to reckless behavior that kills and injures not just drinkers but those around them. cost of the condition

The condition part of the problem is binge drinking; the cost is death and injury. If bingeing had no cost, it would be no problem. Readers have to see the condition and cost *together* before they see the whole problem.

Two Kinds of Problems: Practical and Conceptual   Now it gets complicated, because there are two kinds of problems that motivate readers in different ways. You have to write about them differently.

- One kind of problem is common in the world of practical affairs, so we'll call it *practical*. Practical problems involve what we *do*. Binge drinking is a practical problem.
- The other is more commonly written about in the academic world; we'll call it *conceptual*. Conceptual problems involve what we *think*. That we don't know why students binge is a conceptual problem.

Practical Problems: What We Should Do   Binge drinking is a practical problem for two reasons: First, it involves what students *do*. To solve it, someone must *act* differently. Second, it exacts palpable costs that make (or should make) readers unhappy. If we can't avoid a practical problem, we must *do* something in the world to change the condition, in order at least to ameliorate or at best to eliminate its costs.

We usually name a practical problem in a word or two: *cancer, unemployment, binge drinking*. But those terms name only its *condition*: they say nothing about costs. Most conditions sound like trouble, but *anything* can be the condition of a problem if its palpable costs make you unhappy. If winning the lottery made you suffer the loss of friends and family, it would be a practical problem.

You may think that the costs of a problem like bingeing are too obvious to state, but you cannot count on readers to see the problem as you do. Some readers may see different costs: where you see death and injury, a university publicist might see only bad press: *Those binge drinking students make us look like a party school, which hurts our image with parents.* More callous readers might see no costs at all: *So what if college students injure or kill themselves? What's that to me?* If so, you have to figure out how to make such readers see that those costs affect them. If you can't describe the costs you see so that they matter *to your readers*, they have no reason to care about what you've written.

Writers outside the academic world often address practical problems, but most writers inside it address conceptual ones.

Conceptual Problems: What We Should Think   A conceptual problem has the same two parts as a practical one, a condition and its costs. But beyond that, the two problems are very different.

- the condition of a conceptual problem is always *something that we do not know or understand.*

We can express the condition of a conceptual problem, what readers don't know, as a question: *How much does the universe weigh? Why does the hair on your head keep growing but the hair on your legs doesn't?*

- The cost of a practical problem is the unhappiness we feel from pain, suffering, and loss; the cost of a conceptual problem is the dissatisfaction we feel because we don't understand something important to us.

We can express the cost of a conceptual problem as something more important that readers don't know, as *another, larger question*:

Cosmologists do not know how much the universe weighs. condition *So what?* Well, if they knew, they might figure out something more important: Will time and space go on forever, or end, and if they do, when and how? cost/larger question

Biologists don't know why some hair keeps growing and other hair stops. _{condition} *So what?* If they knew, they might understand something more important: What turns growth on and off? _{cost/larger question}

That larger question may also involve something readers do not know how to do:

Administrators do not know why students underestimate the risks of binge drinking. _{condition} *So what?* If they knew, they might figure out something more important: Would better information at orientation help students make safer decisions about drinking? _{cost/larger question}

I know that can sound baffling: the cost of one question is yet another question. It is why students new to academic writing find conceptual problems hard to grasp. Think of it like this: for a conceptual problem, you answer a small question so that your answer contributes to answering a larger, more important one. Readers are motivated because your small question inherits its importance from that larger one.

> *Here's the point:* Like your readers, you will usually be more motivated by a large question, such as *Why do young people knowingly engage in dangerous behavior?*, than by a smaller one like *Why do bingers ignore known risks?* But you can't begin to answer a question as large as the one about dangerous behavior in three, five, or even a hundred pages. So you have to find a question you *can* answer. When you plan a paper, look for a question that is small enough to answer but is also connected to a question large enough for you and your readers to care about.

Part 3: Stating the Solution   Practical and conceptual problems also differ in their solutions. We solve practical problems with action: readers (or someone) must *change what they do*. We solve conceptual problems with information: readers (or someone) must *change what they think*. Your answer to a small question then helps readers understand a larger one: *How much does the universe weigh? Well, it weighs _____. Now that we know that, we can answer a more important question: What is the fate of existence?*

Practical Problems   To solve a practical problem, a solution must propose that someone *do* something to change a condition in the world:

> . . . behavior that crosses the line from fun to recklessness that kills and injures not just drinkers but those around them. $_{problem}$ **We may not be able to stop bingeing entirely, but we must try to control its worst costs by educating students in how to manage its risks.** $_{solution/point}$

Conceptual Problems   To solve a conceptual problem, the solution must state something the writer wants readers to *understand* or *believe*:

> . . . we can better understand not only the causes of this dangerous behavior but also the nature of risk-taking behavior in general. $_{problem}$ **This study reports on our analysis of the beliefs of 300 first-year college students. We found that students were more likely to binge if they knew many stories of other students' bingeing, so that they believed that bingeing is far more common than it actually is.** $_{solution/point}$

As Darwin and Einstein said, nothing is more difficult than finding a good question, because without one, you don't have an answer worth supporting.

Prelude

There is one more device that writers sometimes use in introductions. You may recall being told to "catch your readers' attention" by opening with a snappy quotation, fact, or anecdote. What best catches attention is a problem in need of a solution, but a catchy opening can vividly introduce themes central to your problem. To name this device, we can use a musical term: *prelude*.

Here are three preludes that could establish key themes in a paper about binge drinking.

1. A Quotation

"If you're old enough to fight for your country, you're old enough to drink to it."

2. A Startling Fact

A recent study reports that at most colleges three out of four students "binged" at least once in the previous thirty days, consuming more than five drinks at a sitting. Almost half binge once a week, and those who binge most are not just members of fraternities but their officers.

3. An Illustrative Anecdote

When Jim S., president of Omega Alpha, accepted a dare from his fraternity brothers to down a pint of whiskey in one long swallow, he didn't plan to become this year's eighth college fatality from alcohol poisoning.

Preludes are rare in the natural or social sciences, more common in the humanities, and most common in nonacademic writing.

Here, then, is a general plan for your introductions:

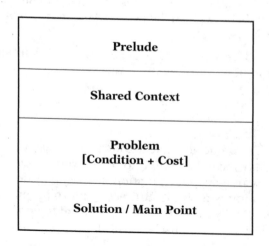

| **Prelude** |
| **Shared Context** |
| **Problem**
[Condition + Cost] |
| **Solution / Main Point** |

Not every introduction must follow that plan exactly. Preludes are optional, and relatively uncommon. In special circumstances writers omit or rearrange other parts as well. Here are four common variations:

- When readers already know the problem well, writers sometimes skip the shared context. When you do this, you lose an opportunity to focus your readers' attention and introduce your key themes.

- When readers already know well both the condition and its costs, writers sometimes skip the shared context and open with the cost before the condition.

- When readers can be counted on to recognize the costs, writers sometimes skip them. This can be dangerous if you overestimate what readers will infer without your help.

- When readers are willing to wait, writers sometimes save their solution/main point for the conclusion, ending the introduction with a promise that a solution will come. Even when readers are willing to wait (which is rare), they are better prepared when they know your main point before they dig into the details.

Although you will find many examples of successful introductions that use these variations, your best option is to follow the general pattern until you have lots of experience with it.

FORECASTING THEMES IN INTRODUCTIONS

In Lessons 4 and 5, we looked at those features that help readers create "local" coherence in short passages, but readers need more to grasp the coherence of a whole document. To help them achieve that coherence, you can use a by-now-familiar principle: begin each document, its sections, and subsections with a short, easily grasped segment that states the point and introduces the themes that readers use to organize the rest. Then, in the body, support, develop, or explain the point and themes stated in the first part.

To grasp the coherence of a document and its sections, readers must see six things:

For the document:

1. Readers must know where the introduction ends and the body begins as well as where each section ends and the next begins. Identify the start of each new section with a heading that includes the key themes for that section (see (5) below). If your field does not use headings, delete them for the final draft.

2. At the end of the introduction, readers look for the document's main point/solution to the problem, which should state the main themes developed in the rest. If you have good reason to save your main point for the conclusion, put at the end of the introduction a sentence that promises the point to come *and* states the main themes.

3. In the body, readers look for the concepts announced as themes at the end of the introduction, using them to organize their understanding of the whole. Be sure that you repeat those themes regularly.

For each section and subsection:

4. Readers look for a short segment that introduces the section or subsection.

5. At the end of that introductory segment, readers look for a sentence that states both the *point* of the section and the specific concepts you will develop as distinctive themes for that section.

6. In the body of the section, readers look for the concepts announced as themes at the end of the introductory segment, using them to organize their understanding of that section. Be sure that you repeat them regularly.

In the limited space we have here, I can't illustrate these principles with entire documents, or even sections. I have to use paragraphs and ask you to analogize the structure of an illustrative paragraph to a whole section of a document.

For example, read this:

2a. Thirty sixth-grade students wrote essays that were analyzed to determine the effectiveness of eight weeks of training to distinguish fact from opinion. That ability is an important aspect of making sound arguments of any kind. In an essay written before instruction began, the writers failed almost completely to distinguish fact from opinion. In an essay written after four weeks of instruction, the students visibly attempted to distinguish fact from opinion, but did so inconsistently. In three more essays, they distinguished fact from opinion more consistently, but never achieved the predicted level of performance. In a final essay written six months after instruction ended, they did no better than they did in their pre-instruction essays. Their training had some effect on their writing during the instruction period, but it was inconsistent, and six months after instruction it had no measurable effect.

The first few sentences introduce the rest, but we don't see in them the key concepts that follow: *inconsistently, never achieved, no better, no measurable effect*. Those terms are crucial to the *point* of the whole and help organize the rest. Worse, we don't get to that point until we get to the end of the passage: training had no long-term effect. And so as we read, the passage seems to ramble, until the end, when we learn what we need to know to make sense of it retrospectively. But that takes more effort than we should have to expend.

Compare this version:

2b. In this study, thirty sixth-grade students were taught to distinguish fact from opinion. They did so successfully during the instruction period, but the effect was inconsistent and less than predicted, and six months after instruction ended, the instruction had no measurable effect. In an essay written before instruction began, the writers failed almost completely to distinguish fact from opinion. In an essay written after four weeks of instruction, the students visibly attempted to distinguish fact from opinion, but did so inconsistently. In three more essays, they distinguished fact from opinion more consistently, but never achieved the predicted level of performance. In a final essay written six months after instruction ended, they did no better than they did in their pre-instruction essay. We thus conclude that short-term training to distinguish fact from opinion has no consistent or long-term effect.

In (2b), we quickly grasp that the first two sentences introduce what follows. And in the second sentence, we see two things: both the point of the passage and its key terms.

> 2b. In this study, thirty sixth-grade students were taught to distinguish fact from opinion. <u>They did so successfully during the instruction period, but the **effect was inconsistent and less than predicted,** and six months after instruction ended, the instruction had **no measurable effect.**</u> <small>point of the passage</small>

Consequently, we feel the passage hangs together better and we read it with more understanding.

We can look at only short passages to illustrate these principles, but you can imagine how they apply to longer sections and whole documents. Imagine two documents: in one, the point of each section and the whole appears at its *end* [as in (2a)] and what openings there are do not introduce the key terms that follow; in the other, each point appears in an *introductory* segment to every paragraph, section, and of the whole [as in (2b)]. Which would be easier to read and understand? The second, of course.

Keep in mind this principle: put the point sentence at the *end* of the short opening segment; make it the *last* sentence that your reader reads before starting the longer, more complex segment that follows.

- In a paragraph, the introductory segment might be just a single sentence, so by default, it will be the last sentence readers read before they read what follows. If the paragraph has a *two*-sentence introduction [as did (2b)], be sure the point of the paragraph is the *second* sentence, still making it the last thing readers read before they read the rest.

- For sections, your introduction might be a paragraph or more. For a whole document, you might need several paragraphs. Even in those cases, put your point sentence at the end of that introductory segment, no matter how long it is. Make your point the last thing readers read before they begin reading the longer, more complex segments that follow.

Some inexperienced writers think that if they tip off their main point in their introduction, readers will be bored and not read on. Not true. If you ask an interesting question, readers will want to see how you support your answer.

Here's the point: To write a document that readers will think is coherent, open every section, subsection, and the whole with a short, easily grasped introductory segment. Put at the end of that opening segment a sentence that states both the point of the unit and the key themes that follow. Point sentences constitute the outline of your document, its logical structure. If readers miss them, they may judge your writing to be incoherent.

DIAGNOSIS AND REVISION

To diagnose how well you have helped readers create a coherent understanding of your paper, do this:

1. **Determine whether you are posing a practical or conceptual problem.** Do you want readers to *do* something or just to *think* something?

2. **Draw a line after your introduction and between each section and subsection.** If you cannot quickly locate how you have divided your paper into parts, neither will your readers.

3. **Divide the introduction into its three parts: shared context + problem + claim.** If you cannot quickly make those divisions, your introduction may seem unfocused.

4. **Is the first word after the shared context *but, however,* or some other word indicating that you will challenge the shared context?** If you don't explicitly signal that contrast, readers may miss it.

5. **Divide the problem into two parts: condition and cost.**
   a. **Is the condition the right kind for the problem?**
   - For a practical problem, the condition can be whatever exacts a palpable cost.
   - For a conceptual problem, the condition must be something not known or understood. Don't state it as a direct question, *What causes bingeing?*, but as a statement of what we do not know: *But we do not know why bingers ignore known risks.*
   b. **Does the cost appropriately answer *So what?***
   - For a practical problem, the answer to *So what?* must state some palpable cost that causes unhappiness.
   - For a conceptual problem, the answer to *So what?* must state some more significant issue that is not known or understood.

6. **Underline your solution/claim and circle its most important words.** It should be the main point of your paper and the circled words should state the key concepts that the rest of your paper will develop as themes.

7. **In the body of the paper, circle the key themes and other words that refer to the same concepts.** If you cannot find where your paper has repeated its connecting ideas, neither will your readers.

8. **Draw a line after the introductory segment of each section and subsection.** If you cannot quickly locate where you set up a section, neither will your readers.

9. **Underline the sentence(s) that state(s) the main point of the section and box its most important words that you did not circle in step 7.** That point is what the rest of the section will support and the boxed words are the key concepts that the section will develop as its distinct themes.

10. **In the body of the section, put a box around that section's themes and other words that refer to the same concepts.** If you cannot find where your section has repeated its connecting ideas, neither will your readers.

This lesson does not cover all that you can do to help your readers create a coherent understanding of your paper, but if you get your beginnings right, you will take your readers most of the way home. As Gabriel García Márquez put it,

> One of the most difficult things [to write] is the first paragraph. I have spent many months on a first paragraph, and once I get it, the rest just comes out very easily. In the first paragraph you solve most of the problems with your book. The theme is defined, the style, the tone.

10

The Ethics of Style

*Ethics is in origin the art of recommending to others the
sacrifices required for cooperation with oneself.*
—BERTRAND RUSSELL

BEYOND POLISH

It is easy to think that style is just the polish that makes a sentence
go down smoothly, but more than easy reading is at stake in
choosing subjects and verbs in these two sentences:

1a. **Shiites and Sunnis** DISTRUST one another because **they** HAVE
ENGAGED in generations of cultural conflict.

1b. **Generations of cultural conflict** HAVE CREATED distrust between
Shiites and Sunnis.

Which sentence more accurately reflects what causes the distrust
between the two—their deliberate actions, as in (1a), or, as in (1b),
the circumstances of their history? Such a choice of subjects and
verbs even implies a philosophy of human action: do we freely
choose to act, or do circumstances cause us to? Later, we'll look at
the way this issue plays itself out in our own Declaration of
Independence.

Our choice of what kind of character to tell a story about—people or their circumstances—involves more than ease of reading, even more than a philosophy of action, because every such choice also has an ethical dimension.

THE ETHICAL RESPONSIBILITIES OF WRITERS AND READERS

In the last nine lessons, I have emphasized the responsibility writers owe readers to write clearly. But readers also have a responsibility to read closely enough to understand ideas too difficult for Dick-and-Jane sentences. It would be impossible, for example, for an engineer to revise this into language clear to everyone:

> The drag force on a particle of diameter d moving with speed u relative to a fluid of density p and viscosity μ is usually modeled by $F = 0.5C_D u^2 A$, where A is the cross-sectional area of the particle at right angles to the motion.

Most of us do work hard to understand—at least until we decide that a writer failed to work equally hard to help us understand or, worse, has deliberately made our reading more difficult than it has to be. Once we decide that a writer is careless, lazy, or self-indulgent—well, our days are too few to spend them on those indifferent to our needs.

But that response to gratuitous complexity only reemphasizes how responsible we are to write clearly, for it seems axiomatic that if we don't want others to impose carelessly complex writing on us, then we ought not impose it on others. If we are socially responsible writers, we should make our ideas no simpler than they deserve, but no more difficult than they have to be.

Responsible writers follow a rule whose more general theme you probably recognize:

> Write to others as you would have others write to you.

Few of us violate that principle deliberately. It's just that we are all inclined to think that our own writing is so clear that when our readers struggle to understand, the problem is not our flawed writing but their shallow reading.

But that's a mistake, because if we underestimate our readers' real needs, we risk losing more than their attention. We risk losing what writers since Aristotle have called a reliable *ethos*—the character that readers infer from our writing: Does our writing make them think we are difficult or accessible? Trustworthy or deceitful? Amiably candid or impersonally aloof?

Over time, the ethos we project in individual pieces of writing hardens into our reputation. So it's not just altruistically generous to go an extra step to help readers understand. It's pragmatically smart, because we tend to trust most a writer with a reputation for being thoughtful, reliable, and considerate of her readers' needs.

But what is at stake here is more than just reputation: it's the ethical foundations of a literate society. We write ethically when, as a matter of principle, we would trade places with our intended readers and experience the consequences they do after they read our writing. Unfortunately, it's not quite that simple. How, for example, do we judge those who write opaquely without knowing they do; or those who knowingly write that way and defend it?

Unintended Obscurity

Those who write in ways that seem dense and convoluted rarely intend to do so. For example, I do not believe that the writers of this next passage *knowingly* wrote it as unclearly as they did:

> A major condition affecting adult reliance on early communicative patterns is the extent to which the communication has been planned prior to its delivery. Adult speech behaviour takes on many of the characteristics of child language, where the communication is spontaneous and relatively unpredictable.
>
> —E. Ochs and B. Schieffelin,
> *Planned and Unplanned Discourse*

That means (I think),

> When we speak spontaneously, we rely on patterns of child language.

The authors might object that I have oversimplified their idea, but those eleven words express what I remember from their forty-four, and what really counts, after all, is not what we understand *as* we read, but what we remember the next day.

The ethical issue here is not those writers' willful indifference, but their innocent ignorance. In that case, when writers don't know better, readers have the duty to meet another term of the reader-writer contract: we must not just read carefully, but when given the opportunity, respond candidly and helpfully. I know many of you think that right now you do not have the standing to do that. But one day, you will.

Intended Misdirection

The ethics of writing are clearer when writers knowingly use language not to further their readers' interests but to disguise their own.

Example #1: Who Erred?   A few years ago, the Sears Company was accused of overcharging for automobile repairs. It responded with an ad saying,

> With over two million automotive customers serviced last year in California alone, mistakes may have occurred. However, Sears wants you to know that we would never intentionally violate the trust customers have shown in our company for 105 years.

In the first sentence, the writer avoided mentioning Sears as the party responsible for mistakes. He could have used a passive verb:

> . . . mistakes **may have been made.**

But that would have encouraged us to wonder *By whom?* Instead, the writer found a verb that moved Sears offstage by saying mistakes just "occurred," seemingly on their own.

In the second sentence of that ad, though, the writer focused on *Sears*, the responsible agent, because he wanted to emphasize its good intentions.

> **Sears** . . . would never intentionally violate . . .

If we revise the first sentence to focus on Sears and the second to hide it, we get a different effect:

> When we serviced over two million automotive customers last year in California, we made mistakes. However, you should know that no intentional violation of 105 years of trust occurred.

That's a small point of stylistic manipulation, self-interested but innocent of any malign motives. This next one is more significant.

Example #2: Who Pays?   Consider this letter from a natural gas utility telling me and hundreds of thousands of other customers that it was raising our rates. (The topic/subject in every clause, main or subordinate, is boldfaced.)

> **The Illinois Commerce Commission** has authorized a restructuring of our rates together with an increase in Service Charge revenues effective with service rendered on and after November 12, 1990. **This** is the first increase in rates for Peoples Gas in over six years. **The restructuring of rates** is consistent with the policy of the Public Utilities Act that **rates for service to various classes of utility customers** be based upon the cost of providing that service. **The new rates** move revenues from every class of customer closer to the cost actually incurred to provide gas service.

That notice is a model of misdirection: after the first sentence, the writer never begins another with a human character, least of all the character whose interests are most at stake—me, the reader. He (or perhaps she) mentions me only twice, in the third person, never as a topic/agent/subject:

> . . . for service to various classes of utility **customers**
>
> . . . move revenues from every class of **customer**

The writer mentions the company only once, in the third person, and not as a responsible topic/agent/subject:

> . . . increase in rates for **Peoples Gas**

Had the company wanted to make clear who the real "doer" was and who was being done to, the notice would have read more like this:

> According to the Illinois Commerce Commission, **we** can now charge **you** more for your gas service after November 12, 1990. **We** have not made **you** pay more in over six years, but under the Public Utilities Act, now **we** can.

If the writer *intended* to deflect responsibility, then we can reasonably charge him with breaching the First Rule of Ethical Writing, for surely he would not want that same kind of writing directed to him, systematically hiding who is doing what in a matter close to his interests.

Example #3: Who Dies?   Finally, here is a passage that raises an even greater ethical issue, one involving life and death. Some time ago, the Government Accounting Office investigated why more than half the car owners who got recall letters did not get their cars fixed. It found that car owners could not understand the letters or were not sufficiently alarmed by them to take their cars to the dealer for service.

I received the following. It shows how writers can meet a legal obligation while evading an ethical one (I number the sentences):

> [1]A defect which involves the possible failure of a frame support plate may exist on your vehicle. [2]This plate (front suspension pivot bar support plate) connects a portion of the front suspension to the vehicle frame, and [3]its failure could affect vehicle directional control, particularly during heavy brake application. [4]In addition, your vehicle may require adjustment service to the hood secondary catch system. [5]The secondary catch may be misaligned so that the hood may not be adequately restrained to prevent hood fly-up in the event the primary latch is inadvertently left unengaged. [6]Sudden hood fly-up beyond the secondary catch while driving could impair driver visibility. [7]In certain circumstances, occurrence of either of the above conditions could result in vehicle crash without prior warning.

(When asked who wrote the letter, I say that it was lawyers for my car company; when asked my car company, I dodge the question.)

First, look at the subject/topics of the sentences:

[1]a defect	[2]this plate	[3]its failure
[4]your vehicle	[5]the secondary catch	
[6]sudden hood fly-up	[7]occurrence of either condition	

The main character/topic of that story is not me, the driver, but my car and its parts. In fact, the writers ignored me almost entirely (I am in *your vehicle* twice and *driver* once), and completely removed themselves. In sum, it says,

> A car might have defective parts. Its plate could fail and its hood fly up. If they do, it could crash without warning.

The writers also nominalized verbs and made others passive when they referred to actions that might alarm me (n = nominalization, p = passive):

failure $_n$	vehicle directional control $_n$	heavy brake application $_n$
be misaligned $_p$	not be restrained $_p$	hood fly-up $_n$
is left unengaged $_p$	driver visibility $_n$	warning $_n$

If the writers intended to deflect my fear and anger at them, then they violated their ethical duty to write to me as they would have me write to them, for surely they would not swap places with a reader deliberately lulled into ignoring a condition that threatened his life.

Of course, being candid has its costs. I would be naive to claim that everyone is free to write as he or she pleases, especially when a writer's job is to protect an employer's self-interest. Maybe the writers of that letter felt coerced into writing it as they did. But that doesn't mitigate the consequences. When we knowingly write in ways that we would not want others to write to us, we abrade the trust that sustains a civil society.

We should not, of course, confuse unethical indirectness with the human impulse to soften bad news. When a supervisor says *I'm afraid our new funding didn't come through,* we know it means "You have no job." But that indirectness is motivated not by dishonesty, but by kindness.

In short, our choice of subjects is crucial not only when we want to be clear, but also when we want to be honest or deceptive.

RATIONALIZING OPACITY

Necessary Complexity

A more complicated ethical issue is how we should respond to those who know they write in a complex style, but claim they must, because they are breaking new intellectual ground. Are they right, or is that self-serving rationalization? This is a vexing question, not just because we can settle it only case by case, but because we may not be able to settle some cases at all, at least not to everyone's satisfaction.

Here, for example, is a sentence from a leading figure in contemporary literary theory:

> If, for a while, the ruse of desire is calculable for the uses of discipline soon the repetition of guilt, justification, pseudo-scientific theories, superstition, spurious authorities and classifications can be seen as the desperate effort to "normalize" *formally* the disturbance of a discourse of splitting that violates the rational, enlightened claims of its enunciatory modality.
>
> —Homi K. Babba

Does that sentence express a thought so complex, so nuanced that its substance can be expressed only as written? Or is it academic babble? How do we decide whether in fact his nuances are, at least for ordinarily competent readers, just not accessible, given the time most of us have to figure them out?

We owe readers an ethical duty to write precise and nuanced prose, but we ought not assume that they owe us an indefinite amount of their time to unpack it. If we choose to write in ways that we know will make readers struggle—well, it's a free country. In the marketplace of ideas, truth is the prime value, but not the only one. Another is what it costs us to find it.

In the final analysis, I can suggest only that when writers claim their prose style must be difficult because their ideas are new, they are, as a matter of simple fact, more often wrong than right. The philosopher of language Ludwig Wittgenstein said,

> Whatever can be thought can be thought clearly; whatever can be written can be written clearly.

I'd add a nuance:

> . . . and with just a bit more effort, more clearly still.

Salutary Complexity/Subversive Clarity

There are two more defenses of complexity: one claims that complexity is good for us, the other that clarity is bad.

As to the first claim, some argue that the harder we have to work to understand what we read, the more deeply we think and the better we understand. Everyone should be happy to know that no evidence supports so foolish a claim, and substantial evidence contradicts it.

As to the second claim, some argue that "clarity" is a device wielded by those in power to mislead us about who really controls our lives. By speaking and writing in deceptively simple ways, they say, those who control the facts dumb them down, rendering us unable to understand the complex truths about our political and social circumstances:

> The call to write curriculum in a language that is touted as clear and accessible is evidence of a moral and political vision that increasingly collapses under the weight of its own anti-intellectualism. . . . [T]hose who make a call for clear writing synonymous with an attack on critical educators have missed the role that the "language of clarity" plays in a dominant culture that cleverly and powerfully uses "clear" and "simplistic" language to systematically undermine and prevent the conditions from arising for a public culture to engage in rudimentary forms of complex and critical thinking.
>
> —Stanley Aronowitz, *Postmodern Education*

This writer makes one good point: language is deeply implicated in politics, ideology, and control. In our earliest history, the educated elite used writing itself to exclude the illiterate, then Latin and French to exclude those who knew only English. More recently, those in authority have relied on a vocabulary thick with Latinate nominalizations and on a Standard English that requires those Outs aspiring to join the Ins to submit to a decades-long education, during which time they are expected to acquire not only the language of the Ins, but their values, as well.

Moreover, clarity is not a natural virtue, corrupted by fallen academics, bureaucrats, and others jealous to preserve their illegitimate authority. Clarity is a value that is created by society and that society must work hard to maintain, for it is not just hard to write clearly. It is almost an unnatural act. It has to be learned, sometimes painfully (as this book demonstrates).

So is clarity an ideological value? Well of course it is. How could it not be?

But those who attack clarity as a conspiracy to oversimplify complicated social issues are as wrong as those who attack science because some use it for malign ends: neither science nor clarity is a threat; we are threatened by those who use clarity (or science) to deceive us. It is not clarity that subverts, but the unethical use of it. We must simply insist that, in principle, those who manage our affairs have a duty to tell us the truth as clearly as they can. They probably won't, but that just shifts the burden to us to call them out on it.

With every sentence we write we have to choose, and the ethical quality of our choices depends on the motives behind them. Only by knowing motives can we know whether a writer of clear or complex prose would willingly be the object of such writing, to be influenced (or manipulated) in the same way, with the same result.

That seems simple enough. But it's not.

AN EXTENDED ANALYSIS

It is easy to abuse writers who seem to manipulate us through their language for their own, self-interested ends. It is more difficult to think about these matters when we are manipulated by the language of those whom we would never charge with deceit. But it is just such cases that force us to think hardest about matters of style and ethics.

The most celebrated texts in our history are the Declaration of Independence, the Constitution, and Abraham Lincoln's Gettysburg Address and Second Inaugural Address. In previous editions of this book, I discussed how Lincoln artfully manipulated the language in both of his addresses. Here I examine how Thomas

Jefferson managed his prose style in the Declaration of Independence to influence how we respond to the logic of his argument.

The Declaration is celebrated for its logic. After a discussion of human rights and their origin, Jefferson laid out a simple syllogism:

Major premise:	When a long train of abuses by a government evinces a design to reduce a people under despotism, they must throw off such government.
Minor Premise:	These colonies have been abused by a tyrant who evinces such a design.
Conclusion:	We therefore throw off that government and declare that these colonies are free and independent states.

Jefferson's argument is as straightforward as the language expressing it is artful.

Jefferson begins with a preamble that explains why the colonists decided to justify their claim of independence, based on the surprising idea that revolutionaries must have, and declare, good reasons:

> When, in the course of human events, it becomes necessary for one people to dissolve the political bonds which have connected them with another, and to assume among the powers of the earth, the separate and equal station to which the laws of nature and of nature's God entitle them, a decent respect to the opinions of mankind requires that they should declare the causes which impel them to the separation.

He then organizes the Declaration into three parts. In the first, he offers his major premise, a philosophical justification for a people to throw off a tyranny and replace it with a government of their own:

> We hold these truths to be self-evident, that all men are created equal, that they are endowed by their Creator with certain unalienable rights, that among these are life, liberty and the pursuit of happiness. That to secure these rights, governments are instituted among men, deriving their just powers from the consent of the governed. That

whenever any form of government becomes destructive to these ends, it is the right of the people to alter or to abolish it, and to institute new government, laying its foundation on such principles and organizing its powers in such form, as to them shall seem most likely to effect their safety and happiness. Prudence, indeed, will dictate that governments long established should not be changed for light and transient causes; and accordingly all experience hath shown that mankind are more disposed to suffer, while evils are sufferable, than to right themselves by abolishing the forms to which they are accustomed. But when a long train of abuses and usurpations, pursuing invariably the same object evinces a design to reduce them under absolute despotism, it is their right, it is their duty, to throw off such government, and to provide new guards for their future security.

In Part 2, Jefferson applies these principles to the colonists' situation:

Such has been the patient sufferance of these colonies; and such is now the necessity which constrains them to alter their former systems of government. The history of the present King of Great Britain is a history of repeated injuries and usurpations, all having in direct object the establishment of an absolute tyranny over these states. To prove this, let facts be submitted to a candid world.

Those facts constitute a litany of King George's offenses against the colonies, evidence supporting Jefferson's minor premise that the king intended to establish "an absolute Tyranny over these States":

He has refused his assent to laws, the most wholesome and necessary for the public good.

He has forbidden his governors to pass laws of immediate and pressing importance . . .

He has refused to pass other laws for the accommodation of large districts of people . . .

He has called together legislative bodies at places unusual, uncomfortable, and distant . . .

Part 3 opens by reviewing the colonists' attempts to avoid separation:

In every stage of these oppressions we have petitioned for redress in the most humble terms: Our repeated petitions have been answered only by repeated injury. A prince, whose character is thus marked by every act which may define a tyrant, is unfit to be the ruler of a free people.

Nor have we been wanting in attention to our British brethren. We have warned them from time to time of attempts by their legislature to extend an unwarrantable jurisdiction over us. We have reminded them of the circumstances of our emigration and settlement here. We have appealed to their native justice and magnanimity, and we have conjured them by the ties of our common kindred to disavow these usurpations, which would inevitably interrupt our connections and correspondence. We must, therefore, acquiesce in the necessity, which denounces our separation, and hold them, as we hold the rest of mankind, enemies in war, in peace friends.

Part 3 ends with the actual declaration of independence:

We, therefore, the representatives of the United States of America, in General Congress, assembled, appealing to the Supreme Judge of the world for the rectitude of our intentions, do, in the name, and by the authority of the good people of these colonies, solemnly publish and declare, that these united colonies are, and of right ought to be free and independent states; that they are absolved from all allegiance to the British Crown, and that all political connection between them and the state of Great Britain, is and ought to be totally dissolved; and that as free and independent states, they have full power to levy war, conclude peace, contract alliances, establish commerce, and to do all other acts and things which independent states may of right do. And for the support of this declaration, with a firm reliance on the protection of divine providence, we mutually pledge to each other our lives, our fortunes and our sacred honor.

Jefferson's argument is a model of cool logic, but he artfully managed his language to tacitly incline readers to accept that logic.

Parts 2 and 3 reflect the principles of clarity explained in Lessons 2–6. In Part 2, Jefferson made *He* (King George) the short, concrete topic/subject/agent of all the actions named.

He *has refused* . . .

He *has forbidden* . . .

He *has refused* . . .

He *has called together* . . .

He could have written this:

> **His assent to laws,** the most wholesome and necessary for the public good, *has not been forthcoming* . . .
> **Laws of immediate and pressing importance** *have been forbidden* . . .
> **Places unusual, uncomfortable, and distant from the depository of public records** *have been required* as meeting places of legislative bodies . . .

Or he could have consistently focused on the colonists:

> **We** *have been deprived* of laws, the most wholesome and necessary . . .
> **We** *lack* laws of immediate and pressing importance . . .
> **We** *have had to meet* at places unusual, uncomfortable . . .

In other words, Jefferson was not forced by the nature of things to make King George the willfully active agent of every abuse. But that choice supported his argument that the king was an abusive tyrant. Such a choice seems so natural, however, that we don't notice that it was a *choice*.

In Part 3, Jefferson also wrote in a style that reflects our principles of clarity: he again matched the characters in his story to the subject/topics of his sentences. But here he switched characters to the colonists, named *we*:

> Nor *have* **we** *been wanting* in attentions to our British brethren.
> **We** *have warned* them from time to time . . .
> **We** *have reminded* them of the circumstances of our emigration . . .
> **We** *have appealed* to their native justice and magnanimity . . .
> . . . **we** *have conjured* them by the ties of our common kindred . . .
> **They** too *have been deaf* to the voice of justice and of consanguinity.
> **We** *must,* therefore, *acquiesce* in the necessity . . .
> **We** . . . do . . . solemnly *publish and declare* . . .
> . . . **we** mutually *pledge* to each other our Lives . . .

With the one exception of *They too have been deaf,* all the subject/topics are *we*.

And again, Jefferson was not forced by the nature of things to do that. He could have made his British brethren subject/topics:

> **Our British brethren** *have heard* our requests . . .
>
> **They** *have received* our warnings . . .
>
> They *know* the circumstances of our emigration . . .
>
> They *have ignored* our pleas . . .

But he chose to assign agency to the colonists to focus readers on their attempts to negotiate, then on their action of declaring independence.

Again, his choices seem natural, even unremarkable—*King George committed all those tyrannical acts, so we must declare our independence*—but they were not inevitable. What more is there to say about the style of Parts 2 and 3, other than that Jefferson made the obviously right choices?

Far more interesting are Jefferson's choices in Part 1, the words we have committed to our national memory. In that part, he chose a style quite different. In fact, in Part 1, he wrote only two sentences that make real people the subject of an active verb:

> . . . **they** [the colonists] *should declare* the causes . . .
>
> **We** *hold* these truths to be self-evident . . .

There are four other subject-verb sequences that have short, concrete subjects, but they are all in the passive voice:

> . . . **all men** *are created* equal . . .
>
> . . . **they** *are endowed* by their Creator with certain unalienable rights . . .
>
> . . . **governments** *are instituted* among men . . .
>
> . . . **governments long established** *should* not *be changed* for light and transient causes . . .

The agency in the first two sentences is obviously God, but the last two passives explicitly obscure the agency of people in general and the colonists in particular.

In the rest of Part 1, Jefferson chose a style that is *even more* impersonal, making abstractions the topic/subject/agents of almost every important verb. In fact, most of his sentences would yield to the kind of revisions we described in Lessons 2–6:

> When in the course of human events, **it** *becomes necessary* for one people to dissolve the political bands which have connected them with another . . .

> ✓ When in the course of human events, **we** *decide* **we** *must dissolve* the political bands which have . . .

> . . . **a decent respect to the opinions of mankind** *requires* that they should declare **the causes** which *impel* them to the separation.

> ✓ If **we** decently *respect* the opinions of mankind, **we** *must declare* why **we** *have decided to separate.*

> . . . **it** *is the right* of the people to alter or to abolish it, and to institute new government . . .

> ✓ **We** *may exercise* our right to *alter or abolish* it, and *institute* new government . . .

> **Prudence,** indeed, *will dictate* that governments long established should not be changed for light and transient causes . . .

> ✓ If **we** *are prudent,* **we** *will not change* governments long established for light and transient causes.

> . . . **all experience** *hath shewn,* that **mankind** *are more disposed* to suffer, while evils are sufferable . . .

> ✓ **We** *know* from experience that **we** can *choose* to *suffer* those evils that are sufferable . . .

> . . . **a long train of abuses and usurpations** . . . *evinces* a design to reduce them under absolute despotism.

> ✓ **We** *can see* a design in a long train of abuses and usurpations pursuing invariably the same object—to reduce us under absolute despotism.

> **Necessity** . . . *constrains* them to alter their former systems of government.

> ✓ **We** now *must alter* our former systems of government.

Instead of writing as clearly and directly as he did in Parts 2 and 3, why in Part 1 did Jefferson *choose* to write in a style so indirect and impersonal? One ready answer is that he wanted to lay down a philosophical basis not to justify our revolution in particular, but all just revolutions, a profoundly destabilizing idea in Western political philosophy and one that needed more justification than the colonists' mere desire to throw off a government they disliked.

But what is most striking about the style of Part 1 is not just its impersonal generality, but how relentlessly Jefferson uses that style to strip the colonists of any free will of their own and to invest agency in higher forces that *coerce* the colonists to act:

- **respect** for opinion *requires* that [the colonists] explain their action
- **causes** *impel* [the colonists] to separate
- **prudence** *dictates* that [the colonists] not change government lightly
- **experience** has *shown* [the colonists]
- **necessity** *constrains* [the colonists]

Jefferson echoes that coercive power over the colonists again in Part 3:

- **We** *must . . . acquiesce [to] the necessity*, which denounces our separation.

Even when abstractions do not explicitly coerce the colonists, Jefferson implies that they are not free agents:

- It [is] *necessary* to sever bonds.
- Mankind *are disposed* to suffer.
- It is their *duty* to throw off a tyrant.

In this light, even *We hold these truths to be self-evident* is a claim that implies that the colonists did not discover those truths, but rather, those truths imposed themselves on the colonists.

In short, Jefferson manipulated his language three times, twice in ways that seem transparent, unremarkable, so predictable that we don't even notice the choice: in Part 2, he made King George a freely acting agent of his actions by making him the subject/topic of every sentence; in Part 3, Jefferson made the colonists the agents of their own actions.

But to make the first part of his argument work, Jefferson had to make the colonists seem to be the coerced objects of higher powers. Since the only higher power named in the Declaration is a Creator, nature's God, that Creator is implicitly the coercive power that "constrains them to alter their former systems of government." But he did not explicitly *say* that, much less defend it. Instead, he let the grammar of his sentences make that part of his argument for him.

The Declaration of Independence is a majestic document for reasons beyond its style and argument. The same words that freed us from tyranny laid down the fundamental values that justify the self-governance of all people everywhere.

But we ought not ignore Jefferson's rhetorical powers, and in particular, the genius of his style. He created a relentlessly logical argument justifying our independence, but he also manipulated, managed, massaged—call it what you will—spun his language to support his logic in ways not apparent to a casual reading.

If his end did not justify his means, we might argue that Jefferson was being deceptive here, using language instead of argument to establish the crucial premise to his argument: the colonists were not free to do other than what they did; they had no choice but to revolt.

It is, finally, an ethical issue. Do we trust a writer who seeks to manage our responses not just explicitly with a logical argument but implicitly through his prose style? We would say *No* about the writer of that automobile recall letter, because it was almost certainly *intended* to deceive us. We are, however, likely to say *Yes* about Jefferson, but only if we agree that his intended end justified his means, a principle that we ordinarily reject on ethical grounds.

SUMMING UP

How, finally, do we decide what counts as "good" writing? Is it clear, graceful, and candid, even if it fails to achieve its end? Or is it writing that does a job, regardless of its integrity and means?

We have a problem so long as *good* can mean either ethically sound or pragmatically successful.

We resolve that dilemma by our First Principle of Ethical Writing:

> We are ethical writers when we would willingly put ourselves in the place of our readers and experience what they do as they read what we've written.

That puts the burden on us to imagine our readers and their feelings.

If you are even moderately advanced in your academic or professional career, you've experienced the consequences of unclear writing, especially when it's your own. If you are in your early years of college, though, you may wonder whether all this talk about clarity, ethics, and ethos is just so much finger-wagging. At the moment, you may be happy to find enough words to fill three pages, much less worry about their style. And you may be reading textbooks that have been heavily edited to make them clear to first-year students. So you may not yet have experienced much carelessly dense writing. But it's only a matter of time before you will.

Others wonder why they should struggle to learn to write clearly when bad writing seems so common and to cost its writers so little. What experienced readers know, and you eventually will, is that clear and graceful writers are so few that when we find them, we are desperately grateful. They do not go unrewarded.

I also know that for many writers the pleasure of crafting a good sentence or paragraph is often enough to justify the effort to achieve it. It is an ethical satisfaction some of us find not just in writing, but in everything we do: we take pleasure in doing good work, no matter the job, no matter who notices. It is a view expressed by the philosopher Alfred North Whitehead, with both clarity and grace (my emphasis in the last sentence):

> Finally, there should grow the most austere of all mental qualities; I mean the sense for style. It is an aesthetic sense, based on admiration for the direct attainment of a foreseen end, simply and without waste. Style in art, style in literature, style in science, style in logic, style in practical execution have fundamentally the same aesthetic

qualities, namely, attainment and restraint. The love of a subject in itself and for itself, where it is not the sleepy pleasure of pacing a mental quarter-deck, is the love of style as manifested in that study. Here we are brought back to the position from which we started, the utility of education. Style, in its finest sense, is the last acquirement of the educated mind; it is also the most useful. It pervades the whole being. The administrator with a sense for style hates waste; the engineer with a sense for style economizes his material; the artisan with a sense for style prefers good work. *Style is the ultimate morality of mind.*

—Alfred North Whitehead,
The Aims of Education and Other Essays

INDEX

144